Built on Family:
The Little Italy of
Portland, Maine

Jamie Carter Logan

Dedicated to my family: the past, present, and future

CONTENTS

INTRODUCTION

Initially written as a master's thesis and adapted as a book, this work strives to provide a deeper understanding of life in Little Italy and the key role which family and community played in that day-to-day life while furthering an understanding and appreciation of Italian-Americans' contributions to Portland. The Italians, working in manual labor jobs, literally built parts of Portland. But the physical environment in which their ethnic enclave was located was destroyed in part by the urban renewal movement, and developers continue to tear down buildings to build hotels and parking garages in what was once Little Italy.

Growing up as a descendant of an immigrant family who lived in Portland's Little Italy I heard stories about the area during Sunday dinners at my grandparents' house, attended family celebrations at the now-defunct Village Café on Newbury Street, and attended the annual St. Peter's Bazaar. It became clear during my research for this project that such an experience was not unique to my family, as the Italians of Portland maintained strong family connections that have kept the community strong in the decades after urban renewal first began to destroy the built environment of Little Italy. Though that physical environment is largely gone, the Italian community of Portland remains strong. The emphasis on the importance of and dependence on family, a value brought from Italy, not only allowed the Italians to survive and succeed in Portland, but also allowed the community to remain close for more than a century after Portland's Italian community first began to coalesce in the India Street area.

The research undertaken for this work focused on the streets in the India Street area, also known as the eastern waterfront. Though Italians also lived further up Munjoy Hill I limited research to the India Street neighborhood, rather than expand to Munjoy Hill and other areas of Portland such as East Deering. Munjoy Hill is geographically close to the India Street neighborhood, abutting it, in fact, but the two are distinct neighborhoods. At one interview, I asked the spouse of an interviewee if she had grown up in the India Street area as well, and the spouse replied that no, she had grown up on Munjoy Hill.

While using the census records and street directory records of the India Street area for research it became clear that Italian names were not familiar to Portlanders in the first part of the 20th century, and that many names in Portland's City Directories in 2014 have undergone changes since they were first listed in Portland. The misspellings and changes over time could have resulted from several causes: the people the names belonged to were illiterate, the census takers did not know how to spell names, or the families themselves changed the names over time. Even family members themselves are unaware of reasons for name changes:

Mary: My Uncle, John Ricci, went by

Riccio because on my grandfather's papers it's Riccio, but then someone explained it to me like you'd come into New York and when you'd go through customs they'd ask you your name, you'd say Ricci, but they're American and you have a strong Italian accent, they wouldn't understand, and they'd go "Ricci, Ricci, Riccio" ...

Evelyn: I was told there was an argument in the family and the grandfather took the o off of Ricci, and the ones on Newbury Street were Riccios.[1]

As a result, in transcribing the census records for research I typed them out as I could read the handwriting. In some cases, there is an alternate spelling in parentheses next to a name. In this case, such, as Furanti/Ferrante, or DiMatthew/DiMatteo, it is because the latter name is well known in Portland and appears in street directories, obituaries, articles, and other data about Little Italy. The first names of family members also often change from census to census, but are close enough with an understanding of the language barrier and Americanization of names that took place that it is possible to recognize these are the same families.

As with names, the addresses seem to vary from census year to census year, or are different in the street directory than on the census, though often only from 2-4 street numbers. This can be attributed to human error in the case of recognizing apartment numbers in cramped buildings, or to unclear numbering systems. Additionally, as is noted in many instances on the tax records on the Maine

Memory Network[2], many locations had differing addresses, and that is noted on the website, as with:

> 2-6 Middle Street in East End, Portland, was owned by Raffaele Vacchiano in 1924. An alternate name or address for this property was 14-16 Hancock Street. The property was also owned by Anella C. Vacchiano.[3]

It is unfortunate that the above caveats are necessary, as it demonstrates the impossibility of complete accuracy in an investigation of Portland's Little Italy. Cross-referencing sources such as city directories, census records, and personal interviews, it was possible to verify facts such as names, jobs, and addresses. By using a variety of sources ranging from census data to oral history interviews to compiled family history books to newspaper and city reports, it is possible to provide a well-researched and well-rounded study of this vibrant neighborhood.

This study differs from the prior research on Portland's Italians in that it focuses on one neighborhood in Portland, and not the state as a whole. As a result, it delves more deeply into the cultural factors, such as family and a close-knit community, and the fact that from home to work, the daily lives of Italians were marked by family relationships and a community that was, and continues to be, bound by those relationships despite the destruction of the physical environment in which those relationships were formed and strengthened in the United States.

ITALIAN SETTLEMENT IN THE INDIA STREET NEIGHBORHOOD

The India Street neighborhood of Portland, Maine is the oldest section of the city and is extremely important in the city's history. The man oft-cited as the city's founder, George Cleeve, built his home in the area, and poet Henry Wadsworth Longfellow was born in the area. One of the only spots to survive the 1775 British bombing of the city (one of four burnings of Portland) was Alice Greele's tavern at the corner of India and Congress Streets. The site of the colonial tavern is, today, home to a Rite Aid drug store, reflecting the city's transformation that obscures Portland's historic buildings even in the city's oldest neighborhood.

In the first half of the twentieth century, the area was home to a large number of Italian immigrants, and was known as Portland's own Little Italy. Though the Italians settled in various areas in and around Portland, including across the bridge in South Portland, the neighborhood surrounding India Street, the streets near the base of Munjoy Hill such as Adams Street, Munjoy Hill itself, and streets in East Deering such as Veranda and Arcadia, the area of Portland most associated with Italian immigration is that "hardscrabble"[4] neighborhood surrounding India Street. In 1940, the authors of the *Portland City Guide* observed that: "The Italians remained in the vicinity of lower Middle Street, and their colony includes the area from Congress Street south to the waterfront and from Pearl Street east to Waterville Street..."[5] Within these boundaries the streets the Italians settled on in large numbers include: Vine, Deer, Chatham, Franklin, India, Newbury, Hampshire, Middle, Fore, Hancock, Mountfort, and Federal. The areas of Fore, Middle, Federal, and Newbury in which the Italians settled were those sections of the streets located closest to the East End.

Vine, Deer, and Chatham Streets were the very heavily concentrated areas of Italian residences, but following the demolition of those streets in 1957,[6] many Italians stayed in the neighborhood and moved only a couple of blocks east[7] where they would still be close to their countrymen, their church, work, and familiar shops. Like the famously Italian North End of Boston, this neighborhood abutted ports and docks as well as downtown business areas.[8] The neighborhood was also near railroad activity, and thus near work opportunities, as were other Italian enclaves in the United States.[9]

Italians began coming to the United States in large numbers in the late 19th century, and though New York and Boston are often heralded for their large Italian-American population and Little Italy districts, the Italian immigrant population also settled in significant numbers throughout Maine. Many who moved to spots outside Portland in Maine worked in the mills in places such as Rumford and Millinocket, or were skilled stonecutters who worked in the quarries in places like Vinalhaven. When Maine separated from Massachusetts and became a state in 1820, there were no more than 20 Italians living in the state.[10] A century later, following the great migration period of Italians to the United States that number grew to an estimated 5,000 Italians living in Maine.[11] Roughly one-fifth of them were living in Portland[12] in the India Street area. The *1940 Portland City Guide* explains the pattern of growth of the city's Italian population:

> Although occasional Italians drifted into Portland prior to 1800, the construction of the railroad from 1837-42 drew many; but it was not until around 1900 that the nucleus of the present Italian quarter was formed. These immigrants and those who have followed came principally from the south of Italy - Sicily, Sardinia, Apulia, and Calabria...[13]

Prior to being home to many of Portland's Italian-Americans, and following its role as an initial settling point for Portland's founders, the waterfront neighborhood surrounding India Street was home to Jewish, African-American, and Irish residents, as well as other various ethnicities.[14] Though the neighborhood's ethnic makeup changed over the course of the nineteenth and twentieth centuries, its working class identity did not change much until the late twentieth century. Even now, the neighborhood is home to the Jewish Community Center, as well as to the original Shaarey Tphiloh Synagogue (though the building is now host to various businesses), located a mere block from St. Peter's Italian Catholic Church. The evolution of the neighborhood is similar to that of other Italian-American neighborhoods in the northeastern United States. As immigrants came to the United States and looked for a place to settle they needed a location close to work and among others who spoke their language and understood their culture. Such neighborhoods tended to be the older parts of cities, and this was true in Portland.[15] As one ethnic group moved up in economic fortune, they would begin moving to other, more prosperous areas of the city. In the India Street area, this movement happened first with the working class Irish who established the neighborhood as an ethnic, working class neighborhood, then with Jewish immigrants, and the Italians then followed.[16]

As the Italians of Portland moved into the neighborhood the area began to be identifiably Italian, though it was not exclusively Italian. As observed in writings on the Vine/Deer/Chatham Street section on the neighborhood: "In the early 20th century one could find 1600 people from 20 countries (mostly Italy and the countries of Eastern Europe)..."[17] The neighborhood fits the pattern of ethnic identification of neighborhood based on businesses in the neighborhood rather than a uniform ethnic population.[18]

The Italians who settled in the working-class, ethnic India Street area were from the poor, heavily agricultural region of southern Italy. This area of Italy is known as the "Mezzogiorno," and consists of the seven regions south of Rome. Roughly 80% of Italian immigrants to the United States hailed from this area that was hard hit by natural disaster in the late nineteenth century.[19] The residents of the Mezzogiorno were looked down upon by their northern Italian countrymen as an inferior race, even after the 1861 unification of Italy.

> The continued backwardness of the southern regions, according to the rationale, was not the fault of the system

of government, but of the prevalence of southern slackers, incompetents, and criminals. The South, often referred to as Italia bassa (low Italy), was declared to be stagnant, while the North, which became known as alta Italia (high Italy), was characterized as progressive. Ultimately, the conclusion evolved that the only useful function the South could serve was to provide cheap labor for the industrialization of the North and soldiers for the nation's military forces.[20]

Italian-American writer Louise DeSalvo goes further, describing that her southern Italian ancestors were viewed by northerners as "primitive, barbarian, animalistic, racially inferior, ignorant, backward, superstitious, degraded, incapable of being civilized, lazy."

In the United States this prejudicial attitude toward southern Italians stuck with them. Italians who arrived during the great migration were not considered to be White, but were also not considered to be Black. The mass immigration of Italians to the United States took place in an era when racial relations were still contentious in the United States, with the mass migration beginning less than two decades after the end of the Civil War, the Italian immigrants would have faced a level of racism coupled with nativism attitudes. As the title of an essay in *Anti-Italianism: Essays on a Prejudice* so succinctly sums up the experience, they were "Between White Men and Negroes."[21] The dark complexion of Italians meant that Italians, then not only had the prejudice against their nationality to contend with, but the prejudice that African-Americans faced as a result of their skin color.[22] This ambiguous place which the Italians occupied in the American racial strata would be a hardship for immigrants trying to find their place in American society, and would certainly have contributed to the insular nature of Italian enclaves. The endnotes for "Perversions of Knowledge," an essay included in *Anti-Italianism* describe such a station in society as "inbetweenness." The prejudice exhibited against Italian-Americans, and the way it was built upon prejudice already exhibited towards African-Americans, as evidenced by such phrases as "black dagoes," meant that both of these groups were faced with an extra level of prejudice because of attitudes held by the establishment classes toward both groups. It also seems as though such attitudes meant that other immigrant groups that one might think would be welcoming to Italians, such as the Irish, due to cultural similarities like the Catholic religion they shared, would be less inclined to be friendly to newly arrived Italian immigrants in part because of the racial prejudice the Italians faced in the wider American society.[23]

With the widespread prejudice against Italians in the United States, it seems unlikely that Portland was immune from it, especially when considering that as late as 1940 the city was still identified as primarily "English-Scotch-Irish."[24] Even in the 1970s the neighborhood was referred to as 'guineatown' by those who did not live there[25] - the same nickname given to prominent Italian-American Frank Sinatra's childhood neighborhoood.[26]

However, interviews for this project do not recall direct prejudice in Portland. Instead, interviewees portrayed any ethnic jabs as childhood taunting, and ethnic labels as not mean-spirited but simply how people identified each other. As Portland interviewee, Evelyn Ricci put it, "And we would fight with them. We called them Jewboys and they would call us Guineas! (laughing)"[27] The generation that those interviewed for this project are of likely impacted their experience, or lack thereof, with discrimination, as they lived during the 1920s-forward. Unlike their parents, they spoke English, attended school, and in some cases married outside of the Italian-American community. Due to certain recorded instances of discriminatory attitudes, it is likely the parents of those interviewed would have been more likely to experience prejudice based on their Italian heritage.

For example, it seems the city made a point to record when the Italian population required attention, specifically recording when the fire department was called to an Italian-occupied building, but not doing the same for other ethnic groups.[28] Such official recording shows that even though as children those interviewed may not have been aware, and may not have dealt with it on a daily basis, the establishment class of Portland still viewed the Italian population and neighborhood as a troubled part of the city's population. The attitude did not disappear, as the eventual slum clearance process would show in the 1950s.

Gregory St. Angelo attributed some of the difficulty his grandfather faced in Portland to such racial and ethnic prejudices: "Many doors were closed to Italians, probably because they were a little darker skinned...and then there was the feeling they were all involved with the Mafia, too."[29] The idea of Mafia involvement is one that pervades the current understanding of Italian-American life, and has only increased with the popularity of movies like *The Godfather* and shows like *The Sopranos*. Anecdotal evidence exists of a Mafia presence in Portland's Little Italy, but hard evidence seems to be nonexistent. One person interviewed for this work described a family known to be involved with Mafia activities, including that they were known to have illegal dealings with Mafia-associated people from New York, but requested that their name not be used. Others corroborated the comments provided by the interviewee, on the condition their confirmation would be used anonymously as well.

Another former resident of Little Italy called to share information after seeing an explanation of this project in the St. Peter's Church Bulletin. The caller revealed that his mother and father moved out of the Little Italy neighborhood because they were frightened of the presence of the 'Black Hand' group and thought that East Deering would be a better place to raise a family. The Black Hand Society, *La Mano Nera* in Italian, was well-known in New York as a group that "used the imprint of a coal-blackened hand to spread the fear that facilitated their criminal activity...the chief targets were prospering immigrants."[30] During the phone call, the caller also explained that his mother was concerned about the presence of bootlegging and he mentioned the 'Casale Boys' - though it is not clear if it is the same Casale family who would later start a construction business - as bootleggers.[31]

It is not clear whether it was mafia-related or not, but gunfights did occur in the neighborhood. Leo Micucci recalled that: "There were gunfights - mostly Italians against Italians. A guy would be scared to drive down Middle Street."[32] With only scant and largely anecdotal evidence available, it is still worth noting that such stories exist about Portland's Little Italy, and that such activity, or even the idea of it that people may have heard of in New York or Boston, may have skewed Portlanders' ideas about Italian-Americans and the enclave in which they lived.

The Italians who lived in the India Street neighborhood settled in an historic neighborhood and turned it into their own. As an ethnic group that was discriminated against in the wider United States and that did not speak English, they needed a neighborhood not only near work, but that also provided an insulated environment in which they could maintain cultural practices. The India Street neighborhood, with its ethnic history, provided that environment, and the Italians of Portland had their base from which to grow their families, earn money, start businesses, and create and sustain a vibrant community.

IMMIGRATION OF SOUTHERN ITALIANS

Before coming to America, the peasants of southern Italy endured harsh conditions, and their lives were not easy even without considering the natural disasters and diseases that assailed the region. They did not own their land, and worked under the harshest of conditions with little to eat or drink. The work days were long, and the labor was intense. It is difficult to understand how the southern Italians were marked as a 'lazy' people when one reads of the conditions they endured to provide even a little for their families. As DeSalvo writes of her ancestors' experience in the region of Apulia (called Puglia in Italian):

> The fields my grandfather worked were seven miles from where he lived. That zappatori - diggers - walked there with their tools on their backs. That they began work at sunrise and left their homes at three or four in the morning. I didn't know that they worked from sunrise until sunset. Then they walked back to their homes, where they'd eat something - bread, softened with

water; in a good year, a few broad beans; some pasta; and whatever their wives or mothers could glean or steal without getting caught...I didn't know that during harvest they were forbidden to go back home. They slept in the fields, without shelter or blankets. Those would have cost money, diminished profits. And besides, these people were used to living like animals...I didn't know that farm workers who ate every day were considered wealthy...I didn't know that workers paid 60 percent interest on loans, so their wages were taken to pay their debts, and they were forced to work only for an insufficient amount of food. I knew that children started working at eight. But I didn't know they worked for half-wages... the emigration of Southern Italians...was a form of rebellion against these harsh conditions...[33]

The southern Italians who arrived on America's shores, as with so many other immigrant groups, were looking to improve their economic situation and to improve the lives of their families. Nancy Jo Polito, whose father came to Portland from Bovino in the Apulia region of southern Italy, writes about her ancestors' experiences: "...they all worked as soon as they were able, pooling their money so they might continue to live together," then she continues to discuss the difficult labor conditions, describing the charcoal business her father's side of the family owned:

They would set up sheds to live in, then cut down the trees to make the charcoal. They would bag the charcoal in 100-kilo sacks, then deliver to homes and businesses. My father told me how heavy the sacks were. He would fill a two-wheeled cart with these sacks, and his donkey would pull as my father delivered coal to various towns.[34]

Polito also makes a point of mentioning how families had to work together to ensure their survival[35] - this characteristic is one that would remain as Italians made their way across the ocean and settled in America. The family ties of Italian-Americans are notoriously strong, and that is partially due to the fact that the difficult life that Southern Italians led required families to depend on one another, and in doing so became protective of their families and village, and they continued to be so even after moving to the United States.

Though family ties were and are an important part of life for Italians, the Italians did not initially migrate as entire families. Instead, the first waves of Italian immigrants were heavily made up of 'birds of passage' - men who would come to the United States with plans to stay for only one season of work, head back to Italy, then return again for another season. Some birds of passage intended to stay in the United States long enough, perhaps even several years, to earn a decent sum, return to Italy with it, and remain in Italy permanently. [36] Researchers estimate that from 1880 to 1921, 78% of all Italian immigrants were men.[37] The phenomenon was so pervasive that the phrase "white widow" was coined to describe an Italian woman whose husband was in America.

However, as evidenced by the growing population of Italians in the United States, it is clear that many who intended to be birds of passage ended up staying in the United States and settling down to raise a family, or sent for their family back in Italy - whether a wife and children, their brothers and sisters, or other relatives - and settled in cities. World War I would have certainly had an impact on those who may have planned to return to Europe, but could not because of travel restrictions and other difficulties caused by the fighting.[38] Whether because they could not return, or did not want to, these men's decision to stay in the United States is what is responsible for creating the Little Italy neighborhoods throughout the United States, including Portland.

The census records for Portland's Little Italy neighborhood demonstrate a high incidence of the common practice of married men immigrating to the United States, then later sending for their wives and children, as well as other relatives. In 1910, 75% of the foreign-born Italians in Maine were men without families.[39] The census listings for this area of Portland are heavily laden with records of boarders, often single or married men who had emigrated from Italy, and boarded with families, likely those they had some connection to from Italy, and who had helped them to find jobs. Oftentimes the boarders are listed in the same occupation as the heads of household (husbands/fathers) in the census information. For example, Severino Nappi and his son Samuel are both employed as oilers at the railroad roundhouse, as is Tony Santrilli who was boarding with the family at their Monument Street home.[40]

The birds of passage and the immigrants who

eventually followed them likely did not come directly to Portland, but rather would have arrived in New York City, or even Boston, then travelled to Portland because they had heard through the community that work could be found there, or because a family member there sent for them. New York City was the primary port of entry, as 97 percent of Italians who arrived in the United States from 1880-1924 first went to New York.[41] Giovanni Amato, the founder of the Amato's sandwich shops, first lived in Brooklyn before coming to Portland.[42] Others may have gone to other parts of Maine from New York before coming to Portland, as a study of immigrants during the period of the great migration notes that: "Many of the Italian laborers involved in building Maine's railways were drawn from the Five Points section of Manhattan."[43] Italian immigrants went where jobs were available, the word then spread about opportunities among families and within the Italian communities. With the jobs available in the India Street area of Portland many ended up there and raised families there, though they may have entered the United States somewhere else and somewhere much more associated with Italian-American culture such as New York City.

Dominic Candelmo came through Ellis Island with his family at age thirteen in 1916, and the family then continued on to Portland where others from their hometown of Vieste had already settled.[44] Dominic and Bridget Colucci emigrated, then lived in New York City before moving to Maine, as did Michael and Mary Grace Paulino and their children.[45] Antonio and Camillia Seo emigrated to the United States, had four of their ten children in Massachusetts, then came to Portland where they lived on India Street.[46] Giovanni Polito's wife, Giaconda Lacivita Polito, and the couple's children followed Giovanni to the United States. Giaconda and the children left Naples on November 1, 1920 aboard the Taormina, and sailed to New York City - not Portland, even though Giovanni was already in Portland. Giovanni had arranged to meet his wife and children in New York City, and upon passing inspection by immigration officials the family traveled together to Portland by train to start their life in America.[47] Likely, the train would have deposited them at the Grand Trunk Railroad Station right in their new neighborhood.

From these examples it is clear that at least the beginning of many family and *paesani*[48] 'chains' did not originate in Portland. However, once here and taking advantage of the economic opportunities offered by the waterfront, railroad, foundry, and other labor jobs, Italians started businesses and sent for their families and *paesani*. For those who came to the United States with the intention of living in Portland, it would have simply been easier and likely more affordable to get passage from Naples to New York and then travel to Portland from New York. Those who arrived with the intention of going directly to Portland did so due to the promise of work, the promise of assistance from *paesani* or family, to meet up with husbands or fathers who had gone before, or some combination of these factors.

An intriguing story of an Italian ending up in Portland because he had been offered help in settling from fellow Italians is that of Emmanuele Cobisi. The story of his arrival in the United States is told in his 1999 obituary:

> At the age of 15 he [Cobisi], left his mother and sister to work at sea...His ship was caught in a storm while still in sight of the coast and capsized. Luckily, all of the crew members were rescued by other vessels.

Mr. Cobisi then transferred to an old freighter, the Saint Joseph, traveling from Italy to Canada and Russia. In February 1931, with Mr. Cobisi now 18, the Saint Joseph arrived in Portland with a load of Russian coal. With offers of help from several Italian men living in the city, Mr. Cobisi decided that the ship could leave, but he was going to stay. Their conversation was overheard by a shipmate and reported to the captain. Mr. Cobisi was quickly locked in a cabin...Mr. Cobisi removed his clothing and escaped the ship through a porthole. So used to swimming in the warm waters of the Mediterranean, he hit the freezing February waters off the coast of Maine and didn't believe he could survive. But he did survive, swimming to Portland's shore and hiding until the Saint Joseph left port.[49]

The obituary goes on to describe how Cobisi worked for the Amatos, a prominent family in Portland's Little Italy, for a time. Italians who came to Portland knew that they were entering a community that was close-knit and that could ease their transition to life in a new country.

This pattern of families and *paesani* following each other to the United States that is so clearly evident in Portland is known as chain migration. In some cases, a man who initially came to the United States as a bird of passage may have found reason to settle instead of returning to Italy. Perhaps he found a steady job, or was able to save enough to buy a house or start a business rather than work as a day laborer and live as a boarder in someone else's home. As the chain migration pattern emerged among Italians in Portland, families followed the same pattern they did in other cities - settling near each other; not only in the same neighborhood, but on the same streets and in the same buildings, and often working with each other, and for each other.

An excellent example of a family chain and its extended reach in Portland is that of the Lorello family. Angelo Lorello emigrated from Italy in 1890 and settled in Portland .Unlike many other Italian immigrants, he brought his wife and child with him when he came to the United States. Upon settling in Portland the Lorellos lived with the Asali family on Chatham Street before moving into a place of their own. His extended family, however, such as his sister Rosa, and the family that she married into - the Villaccis - were brought over to the United States by Angelo after he had established his contracting business and purchased land in Portland. The family history, written for distribution at a family reunion, states that "In 1911, Grandma's brother (a "Lorello") brought the family consisting of Grandma and Grandpa, Aunt Madeline, Aunt Catherine, Uncle Vito and Uncle Fred to the United States." Later, 'Aunt Madeline' would marry into the Valente family, and Catherine would marry into the DeSarno family.[50] The Lorello, Villacci, Valente, and DeSarno families formed a chain of migration into the Portland area and remain connected to this day through those roots that trace back to the late 19th century immigration and life in southern Italy.

Though Angelo Lorello evenutally moved out of Little Italy and began buying land in the Deering area of Portland, branches of the family did live in Little Italy for a good portion of the twentieth century and also owned buildings in that neighborhood. Madeline Villacci, Angelo's niece, had married Michael Valente, and the two bought 41 Middle Street in 1932, where they lived and had both business and residential tenants. Before Michael and his family moved to the area, which his daughter Marie attributed to the need to downsize during the Great Depression, Madeline's parents and siblings were still residing on Chatham Street. The proximity of relatives as well as the easy access to work opportunities and tenants to rent to, was likely a key factor in the relocation to this particular neighborhood. The Villacci family settled on Chatham Street following their immigration in 1910.[51] As they had relatives already in Portland, it was more feasible for them than it may have been for others to emigrate as an entire family. The immigration and movement patterns of these family branches clearly demonstrate how a family member's presence could influence multiple members of their family - often quite an extended family - to move not only to the same city, but also to the same neighborhood.

Another example of chain migration to Portland is that of the Polito family. The Polito family chain began with Antonio Polito's immigration to the United States. Antonio's brother Giovanni then followed him to the United States in 1913, where he worked in a quarry in Thomaston. Giovanni then moved to Portland, opened the Napoli Restaurant in 1919, and his wife and children followed him to the United States in 1920 to join him in Portland. In a comment that seems to sum up how many families ended up where they did, Armand Polito reminisced that, "Meanwhile, my father continued to work in America. Others had gone there too, we knew of a family that had gone before my father..."[52] Leaving Italy to go to America was very common, and knowing that others from their village were there already made it easier for men, and then eventually whole families to make the move.

Once settled in the United States, the family chains continued to expand and intertwine as families intermarried within Little Italy. As was common in other Italian enclaves in the United States, extended families in Portland "shared residences and found jobs and arranged endogamous marriages for members of the family....In America, community involvement was made up networks of many extended families in interdependent relationships."[53] In *Nobody Washes Me, I'm Italian!* Nancy Jo Polito devotes an entire chapter to describing her family tree, and it easily demonstrates how Portland's Italian families are interconnected. In fact, one observation by Polito about her family provides insight into the breadth of the intermarriages in Little Italy and in doing so she highlights the importance of family life for Italians.

> As you can see, my mother and her brother married another brother and sister. As a child, I never really thought about the fact that when I spent time with the Profenno side of the family, my cousins Cammie and Donnie would be in attendance and then when I spent time with the Polito side Cammie and Donnie were there as well.[54]

Intermarriage in Portland was very common, and there are numerous available examples in addition to the the DiMatteo and Profenno families, who were linked by marriage before their arrival in Portland.[55] Marie Valente of Middle Street married Milo Vacchiano, her oldest brother married a Ricci, and another brother married a Pulsoni. Anna Cartonio married Alphonso Russo, and their daughter Mary married into the Taliento family.[56] Mary, Frances, and Carmella Spaltro were three sisters who married into the Nappi, Oddi, and Vacchiano families respectively.[57]

Jeannette Quatrucci married Anthony Galli, who himself was the product of an inter-Italian marriage - Edward Galli and Anna Ricci.[58] James Maiorano grew up on Deer Street[59] and married Josephine Severino, James' sister married an Amato, another sister married a Napolitano, and one of James and Josephine's daughters married into the Romano family.[60] Dorothy Pompeo married Louis Cavallaro and her sisters Marion and Camelia married a Capozza and a Grosso, respectively. Two of her five daughters also married into Portland Italian families - the Ananias and the Capozzas.[61]

The close community and the way in which families spent their lives not only living next door to each other, but sharing celebrations, attending church and school together, and working together certainly lent itself to couples meeting and marrying, as was the case with the Mazziotti couples. In 1996, over 100 family members gathered at the Italian Heritage Center to recognize the joint 50th wedding anniversaries of Dominic Mazziotti and Phyllis DiMatteo Mazziotti, and Dominic's brother Americo Mazziotti and Mary DiMatteo Mazziotti - not only Americo's wife, but also Phyllis' cousin. Both couples had been married in the same ceremony at St. Peter's Church, and had all met at a party in Little Italy when the brothers were home on leave during World War II.[62]

While intermarriage between Italian families was certainly important to the survival of Portland's Italian culture and its persistence today, the trend did change over time. From generation to generation, more and more of Portland's Italians began to branch out, marrying into other ethnicities, notably the Irish. In reference to the Hampshire Street area, Mary Ricci described that: "In that area, Gertie is Irish, Gene Caiazzo's wife was Irish, mom was Irish, Mrs. Feroci was Irish."[63]Though Portland's Italians did begin marrying into other ethnicities, the Italian culture remained a strong factor in these mixed ethnicity families, demonstrating how the family-centric culture of Italians persevered and helped to keep Portland's community close-knit over the course of generations. Mary (Geary) Fasulo was born into an Irish family, but upon marrying she was "thrilled to be embraced by the Fasulo family and learned how to cook Italian dishes from her mother-in-law, Tomasina."[64]

Mary and Evelyn Ricci's mother was also Irish, but they and Mary's daughter still described how a typical Italian Sunday dinner and loud, family-centric household was maintained. Mary Ann's mother, Evelyn, then married a French man, but when interviewed Mary Ann was very firm about the importance of imparting the value of family she learned from her Italian side of the family to her own daughter. It is clear the Italian culture ran deep, and it was clearly the Italian family influence that informed Mary Ann's worldview. Mary Ann's experience is illustrative of how the interconnected families and the tight community in which they lived allowed for the idea of the importance of family to remain as a key element of life over the generations.

LIVING ARRANGEMENTS IN LITTLE ITALY

The living arrangements of Portland's Italians allowed family connections to strengthen. The close-knit, crowded quarters in Little Italy were from necessity, but were also a natural outgrowth of the Italian culture which held family ties in such high esteem. The crowded conditions were not something that disappeared as soon as Italians began to establish themselves in the United States, but remained a part of Italians' lives well into the twentieth century. The physical closeness of extended families in the neighborhood was both a result of the family-centric values the Italians brought with them to the United States, and a factor in the resilience of that culture through several generations of life in the United States.

It becomes clear from census records and even photos of the Little Italy that even if families did not live in the same apartment building, those who lived in the neighborhood did not live far from each other. The streets were narrow, and houses were and buildings were nearly against each other. In spaces where there were not houses or stores there were stables adding to the crowded feel of the area. Even a quick perusal of the City of Portland's 1924 tax records collection shows that stables were quite prevalent in the neighborhood. In fact, the Italian Catholic Church, St. Peter's, was first established in a stable.[65]

One student of the area describes Vine Street: "The street is no more than twenty feet wide with tall buildings on either side, mostly three and four stories coming right up to the sidewalk, forming something of an urban canyon."[66] These 'tall buildings' referred to were primarily apartment buildings and storefronts, with some buildings containing a storefront on the lower level and apartments on the upper level, such as 41 Middle Street and the original Amato's at 71 India Street, both of which were buildings owned by Italians.

By 1924, quite a few of the buildings in the area were owned by Italians, showing that they had made economic strides by this time and were able to save money and purchase homes, businesses, or a building that housed both. Property ownership was enormously important to Italian immigrants and home ownership is what made their extraordinarily difficult manual labor worth it. As Puleo wrote in his study of Boston's Italian community,

> ...owning a home represented the highest form of prosperity for Italians. It meant they could never be evicted by a

dishonest or greedy landlord. It meant
they had acquired an asset that would
have been forever out of their economic
reach in Italy. It meant they possessed a
bulwark against the insecurity of irregular
or seasonal employment or the very real
danger of being injured, or even killed, on
the job. [67]

Owned property could also be passed on to the younger
generation, which both kept property in the family for
economic purposes and provided a reason for families to
remain living nearby one another even as their economic
status improved.

Home ownership among Italians spiked after World
War One,[68] and Portland was no different from the rest of
the country in this regard. The 1910 census shows only two
homeowners of Italian descent in the Little Italy
neighborhood. By 1920 there are roughly forty-three.
Although it was not a large proportion of the Italians in the
neighborhood, it is a significant increase from 1910. By
1930, home ownership among Italians in the neighborhood
had more than doubled to ninety-two with a population of
nearly the same number as in 1920. In 1940 the number of
homeowners has fallen to seventy-four, but the population
considered was also slightly smaller. The 1920s were a time
of great prosperity across the United States, generally, but
with the stock market crash of 1929 came the Great
Depression, and with it, foreclosures. The combination of
the Great Depression, and some Italian families moving into
other areas of Portland by this time likely account for the
decrease in home ownership among Italians from 1930 to
1940.

Oftentimes the owners of a building would rent space to residential or business tenants, and in many cases they were fellow Italians. As a result, the Italian nature of the neighborhood flourished. It was also the frequent case that the owner of the building would not only have tenants, but also boarders who lived with the family. Additionally, tenants renting an apartment would have boarders stay with them to earn extra money. Italians were unique among immigrant groups for the prominent role boarders played in providing family income.[69]

In 1910 the pattern of Italians housing boarders is clearly evident in Portland, and the trend continued through the 1920s. The 1910 census shows many more boarders in Little Italy - all men, all either single or listed as married, but living as a boarder without their wife - and nearly all laborers. At this time, prior to World War I, the birds of passage phenomenon was still strong, and these men would have needed a place to stay that they could not only afford, but where they could communicate in their native language if needed, and be near work opportunities. The homes of their fellow Italian immigrants were ideal, and these households would have needed the extra income.

The number of boarders per household in 1910 was much higher on a regular basis than in later years, and this can likely be attributed to the decrease in birds of passage and increase in settling in America in later decades. As men settled and had families or brought their families to America, they would no longer have been boarders but instead would establish their own households. As the birds of passage trend continued prior to World War I though, it was not uncommon in Portland to have five or more boarders sharing an apartment with a family in 1910, and we see this in the households of the Ferrante family at 85

Fore Street, the Lerttieri family at 28 Newbury Street, the Paulo family at 20 Newbury Street, the DiBiase family who is also at 20 Newbury Street, the Rosario family at 17 Middle Street, and many more.

This living arrangement certainly made for crowded conditions, and that did not change by 1920. In 1920 Rocco and Annie Ricci rented an apartment from the Feroci family at 9 Newbury Street. The Feroci family owned the building and rented apartments, but their tenants also had boarders living with them - four single, Italian men. The Ricci's then had their own boarders living with them - six Italian men. All told, nineteen people lived in these two apartments - the married couples, their children, and the ten boarders.[70] Even if people were not connected directly as blood relatives or through intermarriage, boarding fellow Italians was yet another way in which Italian families became interconnected.

By 1930 the trend of boarders living with Italian families has declined quite a bit. Though one or two boarders living with a family still appear occasionally in the census listings, it is clear that it was no longer a key means of income for Italians in the India Street area. Additionally, as more Italian men began to settle in the United States in the years following World War I, and more families immigrated together, there were fewer single Italian men looking for a place to stay. Instead, Italian immigrants and the sons and daughters of Italian immigrants were living with their own families in apartments in the neighborhood, often not far from their relatives.

However, boarders were not the only reason for the crowded living quarters of Italian families. In Portland's Little Italy it was common for members of extended families to live in the same building, as it was in the Italian neighborhoods of other cities such as Boston and New York. A frequent refrain in memoirs of Italian-Americans is how closely families lived. Louise DeSalvo in *Crazy in the Kitchen* describes how her grandparents lived in the next apartment over from her family in New York City, their "apartments connected by a toilet,"[71] and Martin Amoruso in *Being Italian: A Memoir*, described how he grew up one building over from his grandparents. Amoruso sums up how the close proximity of family members to one another marked Italians as distinct from his peers of other ethnicities: "They visited their grandmothers, we lived with ours."[72] The experience of Portland's Italian-Americans was no different, with stories and government records telling a nearly identical tale of the closeness of families.

At 18 Newbury Street in 1920, Antonio Gilio welcomed his two brothers-in-law into his home. The men emigrated long after Antonio and his wife (their sister), Mary, but the two single men lived in the home with Antonio, Mary, and their four children. One of their children was 23, but as he was working in the shoe factory he was undoubtedly contributing to the family income as he lived with his parents.[73] Economic necessity was not the only reason for Italian families to share housing, as extended families sharing living quarters in the United States was a natural outgrowth of the centrality of family life in Italy. Even as home ownership increased among Italians, it was not unusual for sons or daughters to remain in the same building they grew up in after marrying; living upstairs or downstairs from their parents.

One example of a family who followed this pattern is that of Rose DeRice, the daughter of Luigi and Antoinette Vacchiano Tripaldi. Rose and her six brothers and sisters were raised on Newbury Street. Following Rose's marriage to Joseph DeRice, the couple and their three children lived across the street from St. Peter's Church on Federal Street in one apartment, Antoinette Vacchiano Tripaldi in another, and one of Rose's siblings and their spouse in a third. Gertrude DiFilippo, the daughter of Rose and Joseph, described this living arrangement as "one big happy family."[74] Similarly, Joe Guidi grew up in a building owned by his grandfather. As Joe describes: "My grandfather bought the house. A four family house, he had three daughters. So, three daughters and they all had an apartment plus my grandfather."[75] The 1940 census shows that Joe, his five sisters, and their two parents lived at 18 Chatham Street along with their relatives with family sizes of six, three, and then Joe's grandparents, Frank and Marie Feroci.[76]

In 1940, the close ties of both family and ethnicity were holding strong in Portland's Little Italy, though over a half century had elapsed since the beginning of the great migration. Italians were making gains in purchasing property, but still elected to live among their families and countrymen. The apartments at 73-75 India Street provide a good example of the tight quarters of the apartments in which Italian families lived. Owned by Rosie Shulman in 1924, the tax assessor's records show that the apartment building had a total of twelve rooms with four families living in them.[77] In 1920 four Italian families lived in the building, for a total of twenty-six people in twelve rooms. The families listed are the DiPhillipo family, the Seo family (the building's owners at the time), the Columbo family, and the Viola family. The Seo family is the largest in the building, with eleven family members in one apartment.[78]

A historian of Boston's Italian community comments on the cramped conditions in which Italians lived:

> The homes Italians owned were by no means luxurious. Most were tenement buildings whose apartments may have contained two bedrooms, a kitchen, and a small living room. Perhaps renters had a tiny storage space in a dark, dank cellar. Almost no one in Italian enclaves in the early years, landlords included, had their own bathrooms. Usually, bathrooms were shared and located off a common hallway, and even then, not all of them had showers; immigrants often had to shower in public bathhouses or the YMCA.[79]

Such conditions were not unheard of in Portland. In the India Street neighborhood "many...lived without the modern plumbing and electricity that were, by 1920, so generally widespread as to be considered the norm."[80] In a discussion about growing up in Little Italy in conversation after the formal interview, one interviewee remembered asking her parents for a quarter so that she could walk down to the armory in Portland to use the showers. At the earliest, this would have been the 1930s.[81]

Richard Carter recalled that his grandmother, Madeline Valente, was extremely proud to have her own water heater in the kitchen of their Middle Street apartment. He also recalled the ice man making deliveries so that families could keep their food cold without modern refrigerators. His reminiscences are from the 1960s, demonstrating how slowly such modern luxuries found their way into the apartments in Little Italy, and how important they became once they were available. The 1930 census provides a unique insight into the slow pace at which the Italians' apartments modernized, as it tracks which families owned radios and which did not. While thirty-nine percent of households in the United States owned radio sets by this time, the proportion is much lower among the residents of Little Italy.[82]

When the slow pace of modernization and the number of people living in these apartments is taken into account, it becomes clear that they were not luxurious, spacious living arrangements. However, though the Italians' homes referred to as "tenements" in city documents and in studies of the area such as Zachary Violette's writings on Vine, Deer, and Chatham, the sense of pride Italians had in home ownership meant that these apartments would have been carefully maintained.[83] Though the conditions of the apartments may have been unappealing to native-born Portlanders, the buildings were home to the Italians, and were a mark of pride and achievement particularly for the owners of the buildings. For both owners and tenants, they were important as a place in which they lived among their families and *paesani*.

By living in cramped housing the Italians were both saving money that would later be useful in starting businesses, or even just in feeding their families, as well as perpetuating the strong family ties that were so important to Italian culture. The homes of Little Italy did not have the most space, nor the most modern conveniences, but the people of Little Italy had their community and their cultural traditions, which have been passed down to generations who never knew Little Italy as a close-knit community living in a crowded built environment.

COMMUNITY LIFE

A seminal work on the culture of Italian American communities in the United States is William Foote Whyte's Street Corner Society which studies the culture of Boston's North End (which his subtitle describes as "An Italian Slum") in the early twentieth century. The very title of the work is evocative of the general environment of Portland's Little Italy, as well as Boston's. As Joe Guidi recalled how his father spent the time when he was not at work, "He was out on the street. And that's where everybody was. Out in the street."[84] The southern Italians who came to the United States were from the rural areas - used to working outdoors and spending their lives outdoors. It is not surprising, then, especially when considering the number of people living in small spaces once in the United States, that Italians tended to spend time socializing and gathering outside of their homes on the sidewalks and street corners of the neighborhood. This behavior was a carryover from life in Italy where "social contacts were maintained in the village streets."[85]

Portland's Little Italy was a vibrant neighborhood, with children walking to and from school, women hanging laundry in the yards, men (and some women), walking to and from work, and on Sundays going back and forth from St. Peter's or Cathedral. In the afternoon it was common to see "Italian women swarm the streets..."[86] Men, women, and children also boisterously conversed from yard to porch and from window to street in Italian and English, with all the neighborhood parents looking out for all the neighborhood kids. There were no secrets in the neighborhood, and kids could not get away with anything. The character of Portland's Little Italy cannot be expressed with statistics, or merely names of people and businesses.

Instead, to understand the sense of community, one needs to understand the context in which these Italian immigrants and their offspring lived, conducted business, and socialized. Like the Italian area of Mulberry Street in New York City, the buildings may not have been luxurious, but the neighborhood had a "richness of life and motion and human interest."[87] The sense of community and the social aspects of the neighborhood are a persistent and happy theme that supersede all other experiences in Little Italy for those who lived there. Harkening back to language reminiscent of life in Italy, John Reali remembered a "neighborhood that really was a village, where everyone knew everyone and you saw the same faces day in and day out."[88]

With families living in close quarters, and neighbors being from the same areas of Italy, it is not surprising that the community was so close-knit. After all, that was part of the reason that Italians created enclaves in cities throughout the United States: "In the United States extended families crowded together in urban neighborhoods and continued the ancient practice of aiding their members."[89] Though poor, the community members could count on one another, and the children and adults alike socialized with their peers in the neighborhood. The children played in the streets and parking lots, the adults played cards or gathered outside or around the kitchen table to talk.

At the Ricci family home on Hampshire Street, it was a common sight to see the Ricci men leaning up against the fence, talking to neighbors and passersby, or yelling full conversations back and forth with friends sitting on their porches. Mary Ann Ricci calls this mode of conversation the 'Italian telephone.' Certainly this mode of communication did not fit the stoic Yankee mentality. More conservative Portlanders would likely have been shocked to hear people yelling their business from porch to street, even if it was in a tongue any such (unlikely) passerby were unable to understand. The long-established Portlander would have likely viewed such a scene as a disruption and a commotion, but to Mary Ann and her family, and to the other Italian families of the neighborhood, it was a mark of the closeness of the community and a sign of a vibrantly social life that brought happiness and joy to a population that worked long, hard days.

It was also common for the men of Little Italy to socialize while playing games outside. Games were not only a pastime, but certain games were also a way for the men to maintain a part of their Italian culture in their new home. Rose Valente Carter recalled her father and his friends playing a game as they gathered on the streets of Little Italy before and after work. She described the game as the men throwing out their fingers and guessing what others' fingers would add up to.[90] This game, known as 'La Morra' was common in southern Italy and was brought over to the United States by the immigrants. Such pastimes were regularly seen in cities with large Italian populations such as Hoboken, Long Island, where men played pinochle on the sidewalk.[91] Dice was also a popular game in Little Italy, and it was not unusual to see games being played in the street. [92] Unlike La Morra, however, dice was a game discovered in America and then popularized by the early immigrants who travelled back and forth from Italy, and played it on the voyages across the Atlantic.[93]

Gambling also took place off of the streets, at locations like the Banana Club. The Banana Club was not an open business, and in fact did not even have a sign. Rather, it was a private social club for Italian men located on Middle Street. Owned by Dominic Marino,[94] it was a well-known as a spot for gambling in the neighborhood.[95] There was also gambling on horse racing, which was done by both men and women. It was not formally arranged, but rather depended on the communication lines among people in the neighborhood.

> Evelyn: The Italian men....I remember my father playing, you didn't buy a ticket, it was all word of mouth. You'd pick numbers and then you'd bet the odds on it. It must have been for horse racing I'd guess...I remember my aunt Mary, my father's sister coming in from South Portland, and she'd say Jerry, here's 20 cents...[96]

Music accompanied the background noise of the daily life in Portland's Little Italy and was yet another reason for community members to gather. Marie Valente Maiorino, who grew up in the neighborhood during the 1930s, recalled that enjoying music was a community activity that brought the neighborhood together.

> I was dear friends with Annie Cartonio ... I can remember sitting on the side of her store. She had three steps that entered the back hall. When we were in our teens they used to gather, people came down from India Street, Little Middle Street, and Middle Street. We used to gather on those steps and a man named Mr. Minervino, Steve Minervino, used to play the ukelele and he led us all in song. And we used to sing all kinds of songs. It was a gathering of the teenagers and we enjoyed singing on those steps.[97]

Though the community life of Little Italy was very strong, the Italians of Portland still felt there was a need for an organized social club. The Italian Heritage Center was first established in 1953 and was initially located on Pearl Street on Little Italy. It is now located in the Deering area of Portland, where so many Italians relocated either as they moved up the economic ranks, or because they had to following the demolition of their homes due to urban renewal. The founding members of the club include many who were raised in Little Italy.

Mary Germani Breault, for instance, was the daughter of Gaetano and Assunta Germani, who lived on Newbury Street. Mary, who moved to the Libbytown neighborhood of Portland eventually, not only helped to found the Italian Heritage Center, but also served as its chief cook - certainly not a light task in a culture that holds food in such high esteem.[98] The foundation of the center, like so much else in the Little Italy community, was a family affair, with brothers John and Donato Profenno involved, and both serving terms as club President.[99] The continued operation of the Italian Heritage Center in Portland is indicative of the strong Italian community that is still present in the city and the interest of the members of that community in preserving that community and the Italian culture.

THE WORKING LIFE

The sights and sounds of Little Italy in the early twentieth century were marked by work. In the background of any socializing and children playing would have been a steady stream of industrial noises. The Southern Italians who came to the United States were used to working hard, and were used to manual labor. Once in the United States the Italian immigrants found themselves continuing to do the manual labor they had done in Italy, though in an urban and not a rural setting. In Portland, this meant that they worked for the railroad, on the docks, and in a variety of general labor capacities. As with all else in Little Italy, the working life was marked by family and community connections, beginning with the padrone system which relied on connections among Italians to get Italians to the United States and to find Italians jobs.

The padrone system was made up of labor agents who found jobs for their fellow Italians and received commission from employers and payment from the laborer - from wages, in the form of repayment for their passage to the United States, or some other fee. The padrone system is heavily criticized, and there are many horrible stories of abused and exploited workers, but the *padroni* were also instrumental in bringing Italians to the United States, and finding jobs for those who wanted them. As with other aspects of Italian life, finding work was dependent on community ties.

The padrone system began to take shape in the 1860s, following the passage of a federal law that "allowed the recruitment of immigrant labor under contract." The law then "ended in 1911, when an Immigration Commission Report stated that the padrone system, for all practical purposes, was dead."[100] In his article on the padrone system in Maine, Alfred Banfield admits there are not specific statistics on the padrone system in Maine, but notes that there is evidence of its strong presence in the state. Interestingly, he explains that the padrone system may have not only caused Italians to stay in Maine because they had work, but also because they were essentially "stranded" in Maine when they could not get transportation back to Boston or New York.[101]

Whether they were brought to the United States through the padrone system or not, many Italian immigrants worked in some form of manual labor, especially in the early years of the migration before Italians began to settle and buy homes and businesses. In 1890, one-third of Italians in the United States were classified as unskilled laborers[102], doing work such as pick and shovel work, labor on the railroads, and any number of other jobs that required little to no training, did not require English language proficiency, and often had long hours for low pay. Such work was perhaps not what they expected to find America, but it was not something unfamiliar to the men who first came from southern Italy: "Their peasant background equipped them for this kind of hard work and solid, if somewhat stolid, accomplishment."[103] Little Italy was rife with opportunity for unskilled and semiskilled labor within walking distance, particularly as other ethnic groups such as the Irish began to move up in the economic classes. As a result, the residents of Little Italy did not have to leave the neighborhood, and worked among their family and neighbors.

During the early twentieth century, Grand Trunk Railroad was a major employer in Little Italy. Though all that stands at the site of what was once a large complex is simply one building, Grand Trunk Railroad's impact on the neighborhood and its role in drawing Italian-Americans, and other groups, to the neighborhood cannot be discounted. The physical structure of the railroad's associated buildings was imposing, and the people and goods moved by the railroad were integral to the economic fabric of the neighborhood. As Danielle Gabriello describes in her work *Ghost Street*: "The world of the Grand Trunk anchored India Street and its multitude of small businesses."[104] The Grand Trunk Railroad held perhaps a deeper connection for immigrants who lived in the neighborhood, as it not only provided jobs, but was also the mode of transportation by which many of them arrived in Portland.[105] The loss of the physical structures of Grand Trunk Railroad are also a loss of a part of the Italian immigrants' history.

Working for the railroad could not have been easy work, to be sure, but the census listings and directory listings for Italian-Americans in the first half of the twentieth century reveals that the number of people employed by the railroad is significant.[106] Many of the men listed as employees of the railroad, which was presumably

Grand Trunk, are described as 'laborers' for the company. In 1910, there were twenty-five Italian men from the neighborhood working for the railroad[107], in 1920, after the Italian population in the neighborhood has doubled, there are forty-one men in the neighborhood employed by the railroad,[108] and in 1930, with a barely changed population, there were nineteen men listed as employed by the railroad. In 1940, the railroad employed twenty-three of the Italian men from the neighborhood. Across the years, there are various examples of family members or members of the same household working together at the railroad, such as the father and son Thomas and Sam Botto who both worked for the railroad in 1930.[109] The men employed by the railroad primarily worked as freight handlers and laborers, though one outlier is Henry Aliberti, who had four years of college education and was employed as an engineer for the railroad.[110] Part of the decline from 1920 to 1930 can perhaps be attributed to the fact that in the 1920 census several of the men listed as railroad employees are boarders without families, at least without families in the United States, so it is quite possible that they were birds of passage who left the neighborhood, state, or country. By 1930 employment opportunities in neighborhood businesses, as well as longshore jobs, would have increased in availability.

The center of Little Italy was only a couple of blocks from the extremely active wharves of Portland, making longshore work an accessible option for many Italians in the neighborhood. Longshore work was not always reliable, as it depended on the ships' schedules and the supervisors' choice of who would be on the crew on a given day, but census records show a significant number of Italians employed at the wharves, particularly from 1930 forward. Longshore work was considered semiskilled labor, and as such was not widely available to Italians in the earlier years of their settlement. In the late nineteenth century the Italian immigrants who did work on the waterfront began strictly as freight handlers – a lower paying job than a "longshoreman proper."[111] The growth and opportunity over the years of Italians employed as longshoremen in Portland likely followed the same path it did in New York City:

> Once a sufficient number became longshoremen...an ethnic momentum was set in motion. 'They stood together. Each Italian who found employment brought relatives....If one secured a job as a foreman, he gave preference to his countrymen.[112]

Again, the key role of family and community relationships becomes clear, even at work. In 1910 there are no men from Little Italy working 'down longshore.' By 1920 fourteen of the neighborhood men are working as longshoremen,[113] by 1930 it has increased to twenty,[114] likely due to the influence of family and neighborhood connections. Longshore work was also an environment in which family members and members of the same household worked together, as with the father and son Louis and Anthony Napoleon.[115]   By 1940 the trend of men working as longshoremen has reversed, with only seven longshoremen and one stevedore among the Italian men of the neighborhood.[116]

The increasing availability of factory work to Italians, as well as the Depression's effect on economic activity, likely impacted the number of Italians working as longshoremen.

The longshore work and its unpredictable nature lent itself well to the social nature of the Italian neighborhood. As they gathered on the streets in the morning, the men of the neighborhood discussed which ships were coming in, what cargo was possibly on them, and whether this meant they would have work for the day.[117]

Longshore work was not the only semi-skilled work available to Italians in the neighborhood, as opportunities in the neighborhood included the machine shops, foundries, and forges. Many Italians in the India Street area found work at the Portland Company, Thomas Laughlin, and Megquier and Jones. The numbers of those employed by these companies fluctuated from year to year, but as with other labor jobs, it is possible that the census enumerator listed the work as 'laborer' or 'general work' instead of specifying the place or type of work. In 1910 the number of residents employed in the boiler shop, the foundry, or a blacksmith shop equals six. By 1920, that number has risen to forty-eight, which coincides with the large jump in population during that time period. By 1930 the number has dropped back to sixteen, and by 1940 it drops again to eight.[118] The decreases coincide with a wider availability of careers and increase in education to the Italian population, as well as with a marked increase in those employed as longshoremen and in the manufacturing businesses. As with the city's loading docks, and the railroad, these jobs were easily accessible to the men by foot, and the men of the community would have worked together there. One such example of how the community was close, even at work, is that of Patsey Maiorano, Dominic Amato, and Vincent Troiano who were all employed at a boiler factory, and all lived in the same building at 32 Deer Street.[119] Another example is that of Rocco Delucca and Philip Pallozzo who lived in the same building at 79 Newbury Street, mere yards from the site of Thomas Laughlin, and were both employed as helpers in a boiler shop.[120]

Located just east of Hancock Street, at the current site of the Shipyard Brewery, the Thomas Laughlin Company had a forge, a blacksmith shop, and a machine shop as part of the complex,[121] which provided many opportunities - both skilled and unskilled - for the neighborhood men to earn wages. In addition to providing work for the Italian residents of the area, Thomas Laughlin also provided a memorable backdrop of noise for the neighborhood, so it would have been a constant part of life for the community, even for those who did not work there: "Right next to the Village Cafe where Shipyard Brewery is now was some kind of a foundry or factory. All I remember is that it constantly had this ch-ch-chnk thump noise going on down there except late at night...."[122] The Thomas Laughlin property also provided opportunity for the neighborhood kids to play baseball: "We'd play like street baseball in their parking lot... I still have a little scar I got on the barbed wire they strung up to keep us from climbing the fences. We climbed the fences anyway to go in there and play baseball in the parking lot on a Saturday."[123] The places of work for the neighborhood's Italians were more than that – they were yet another place where the Italians strengthened their community, whether by working alongside their neighbors or by taking advantage of the physical property for recreation with their neighbors.

Though it was primarily men who were employed in Little Italy, some women did work outside of the home. In 1920 it was common for those women who were employed to be working as 'waist makers,' and in later years, the job title of 'stitcher' is often given to women. The trend of

Italian women working in the clothing industry was not a fleeting fad - in 1950 77% of Italian-American women were employed in the needle trades.[124] It was not unusual for more than one woman in a household to be employed in the same work, or for a woman to be employed at the same place as her brother or father.

The daughters of Italian immigrants, particularly those who came of age during the Depression years, often held down jobs both before marrying and after starting their own household. Allan Neff recalled that his mother, a Guidi, worked at the K&M Pants Factory at the corner of Pearl and Middle Streets, along with her mother and all of her sisters.[125] Allan's mother and Joe's mother both had families during the time they worked at the pants factory. At 26 Hancock Street in 1930, Theresa and Jennie Tripaldi, 21 and 18 respectively, were still living with their family and working as stitchers at the pants factory.[126]

It was certainly not universal for Italian women in the United States to have jobs, but it was not unusual. Because the majority of women who are listed as working in the 1930 and 1940 census are listed as employed in factories, it is likely that they would have also been engaged in doing piecework like their counterparts in Boston and New York City[127], or that their neighbors who did not work at the factories would have perhaps done piecework at home. In southern Italy, women learned the needle trades early and they brought these skills with them to the United States, and undoubtedly also passed them on to their daughters.[128]

The men from Little Italy also worked in the factories, though this trend begins to emerge more prominently after 1930. It is possible, however, that those men listed as 'laborers' doing 'general work' in earlier censuses were employed by the factories, even if only for some portion of the year, as even in the 1930 census many of the men listed as 'laborers' are then identified as working in factories. As Italian employment in the factories increased, they again used their close family and community connections to assist their neighbors: "...the few who broke into factory work provided the link to similar opportunities for their own sons and daughters."[129] By 1930 many residents of Little Italy, men and women alike, were employed by the factories, and this remained true in 1940. In 1910, only nine residents of Little Italy were employed by the factories,[130] and by 1930,[131] there were 54 employed by factories. The number only continued to grow by 1940 - rising to 119. This huge increase is likely attributable to more women working outside of the home - mostly the daughters of immigrants, who would have attended some level of school and had a better handle on English than their parents. The handkerchief factory, underwear factory, shirt factory, shoe factory, and pants factory were all listed as places of work for residents of Little Italy.[132]

Though factory work was a primary occupation of women from Little Italy, women did work in other capacities - though often in home-based or family business-based work. Many worked as clerks or waitresses in their husbands' or fathers' or brothers' stores and restaurants, but others contributed to the neighborhood and earned money by serving as midwives or by running the business aspect of the apartments owned by their family. Madeline Valente is an example of a woman who did both midwifery and apartment management. It is hard to believe she would be the only woman engaged in such work in Portland's Little Italy, as midwifery was common among women in their homeland of the Mezzogiorno, where the women who had a hand in such medical work were known as 'levatrici.'[133]

Women served as the managers of apartment buildings in other Little Italies.[134] Interestingly, Madeline's daughter described that Madeline came up with her own system of counting to do the bookkeeping for the apartments, and Louise DeSalvo explained that her ancestors did the same.[135] Italians who had no formal schooling still found a way to track their income and to earn money to build a better life for their children.

The Portland in which the children and grandchildren of Italian immigrants now live looks much different than the Portland in which their ancestors first settled. The physical appearance of Portland in 2014 owes much to the Italian immigrants and their descendants who worked in the building trades, both as owners and employees. Rose Valente remembers the prominence of such work among people in the neighborhood:

> Mostly construction is what I remember, barbershop, I remember. But when I think about it the friends I had, their fathers were mostly construction, contracting, that sort of job...Yes, and bricklayers, that's another thing. They would do that fancy brickwork.[136]

The construction companies for which the Italians of the neighborhood worked were often based in the neighborhood, owned by Italian families, and employed fellow Italians.

As with other workplaces that employed neighborhood Italians, some contracting companies were located right in the neighborhood, not far from their owners' or employees' residences. Joseph Casale's contracting company was based at 48 Middle Street in 1925.[137] Joseph, his wife Camilla, and their five children lived just blocks away at 221 Fore Street.[138] D. Casso and Son General Contractors was named for the owner, Diego Casso, who ran the business from 21 Vine Street.[139] The ad the company placed in the 1925 Portland City Directory touted their development of the Broadway Park Homes in South Portland, which is an interesting contrast to how, at least as perceived by Portland's establishment, the Casso's were not living in the best of circumstances themselves. In 1925 the Casso family owned 19-21 Vine Street, which would later be razed after the Vine/Deer/Chatham neighborhood was determined to be a slum.

Some of the companies did work that was crucial to the physical environment of the Italian community that, unlike parts of the neighborhood, still exist today. For example, C. Galli and Sons, Inc. were hired to build St. Peter's Church. Antonio C. Galli ran the company which was well-regarded outside of Portland's Italian community as early as 1912. The company also did work all over the state, and contributed to Maine on the whole in this way. One of C. Galli and Sons' projects was the construction of the All Souls Chapel at Poland Springs.[140] Because it was such a longstanding company with work throughout the state, the company employed many of Portland's Italian men as general laborers or as masons.[141] Anthony Galli, like his father Edward,[142] took up the family business and worked as a mason contractor for much of his life. He attended St. Peter's Church, which his forebears had built, and married a girl from the Little Italy neighborhood, Jeanette Quattrucci.[143] A life closely tied to the Little Italy community extended, even through work, across generations for Italian families.

The opportunity for the first immigrants in Portland to settle and to find work came in part from a fellow Italian contractor whose company extended over generations in Portland. Camillo Profenno came to the United States from Lettomanoppello, Italy with his wife Sabia.[144] Camillo's business success allowed him to help out new immigrants who "sought him out for jobs, loans, or any other help they needed."[145]

The Profenno family is also an example of how the trend of close family connections through intermarriage in Portland's Italian community extended to the contracting businesses. All aspects of life truly were tied together through family for the residents of Little Italy. Camillo Profenno's wife, Sabia DiMatteo Profenno, is the aunt of George DiMatteo, who ran the DiMatteo contracting company.[146] George D. DiMatteo, like Donato Profenno, Camillo's son, served as president of the statewide organization Associated General Contractors.

As with the Profenno contracting company, C. D'Alfonso and Son was a contracting company that was owned by members of the same family over the course of generations. The business was located in Little Italy at 47 Adams Street, a building owned by D'Alfonso as early as 1930.[147] Costantino D'Alfonso started the company in 1943, 13 years after he began working as a contractor, and the business was later handed down to his son Samuel, and upon Samuel's death on the job, to Nunzio D'Alfonso, who oversaw the business until 1998.[148]

Though contracting businesses had their names attached to projects, and in doing so brought the Italians' contributions to Portland's physical landscape to the public's attention, many more Italians contributed to the construction of Portland as it now exists by doing backbreaking labor – street work, railroad work, unskilled building trades work, and whatever other unskilled labor they could find. From 1910 to 1940, manual labor remained a key aspect of life for Portland's Italians. In 1910, most Italians were earning money through general labor, but by 1940 some of those employed as laborers worked for the city or were employed by the Works Progress Administration as laborers on sewer projects.

Emilio Ferrucci came to the United States and worked building the stone culverts under Baxter Boulevard, work described as "menial and backbreaking."[149] Joe Guidi, who grew up to be a successful businessman in Portland, described during an interview how his father provided for his family by helping to build the streets of Portland we know now:

> You know what pick and shovel is? You know when they dig a hole up in the street? They have these machines that dig the holes. Years ago they didn't have machines. My father was down there digging the holes.[150]

Pick and shovel was certainly a labor-intensive, dirty job, but it was a job, and the Italians of Portland did not shy from it, even after they had been in the United States for more than a generation. The railroad employed men to do pick and shovel work,[151] and Italians on the census were listed as pick and shovel workers who did 'construction' work, or simply as laborers whose more specific job was pick and shovel, some perhaps employed by the city or by construction companies contracted out by the city.

Other Italians worked as hod carriers, assisting stonemasons, bricklayers, and others at worksites. The Merriam-Webster Dictionary defines a hod as: "a tray or trough that has a pole handle and that is borne on the shoulder for carrying loads (as of mortar or brick)"[152] It is quite likely that hod carriers were employed by other Italians who owned contracting companies, and that some of these men turned what they learned during their time as hod carriers into a construction business of their own.[153]

From hod carriers to business owners, the Italians of Portland were instrumental in constructing the physical environment of the city. In doing the work, they maintained and grew family and community connections that helped their community to flourish, while contributing to the physical environment of the city even as the decision-makers of the city would determine that Little Italy's buildings needed to be demolished.

Family businesses extended beyond construction to delivery businesses. The J. Pallota Company was one such business based in Little Italy. Though they advertised as specializing in 'bag coal' and 'wood' they also delivered ice. Pallotta bought the business from Vito Villacci, another Italian immigrant in the neighborhood, again showing the longstanding connections between families in the neighborhood. As Vito's daughter Madeline explained: "Papa had a coal and wood business which he sold bagged door-to-door with a horse and buggy...Papa cut his hand on his saw so he sold his business to a friend, Joe Pallotta. His wife and he were my godparents.[154] The Villacci family then moved to Falmouth, but the delivery company under Pallotta remained located at 1 and 5 Mountfort Street in 1925.[155] By 1951 there is a listing in the Portland Street Directory for J. Pallotta Oil Company, touted as being established in 1928.[156] Pallotta transitioned his delivery businesses into one focusing solely on oil, and as the company grew it relocated to Exchange Street. The company did move out of Little Italy, but it remained a family business.

The business eventually provided a living for Pallotta's son - also named Joseph. The younger Joseph not only remained employed in the family business that had made a name for itself in Little Italy, but also married another child of Little Italy - Concetta Risbara.[157] After the older Joseph Pallotta transferred his business solely to oil his brother Neal appears to have taken over the wood and coal portions of it. Neal's business was located on the other side of India Street from Joseph's Mountfort Street location, at 22 Hampshire Street.[158] Though Pallotta had transitioned to only oil, in 1945 there were still wood dealers in the neighborhood. Samuel Depollo (DiPaolo) and Carrelo Feroci both ran such a company.[159]

In addition to specific labor jobs taken on by Italians, such as delivery work, railroad work, or longshore work, the census records are full of men who described their jobs as 'laborer' and as doing 'general work' or 'odd jobs.' In 1910, fifty men were listed as working at odd jobs, and thirty-six were listed as doing general work. In 1920, there were twenty-five men doing general work and five were working at odd jobs. By 1930, only twelve are working at odd jobs and seven at general work. In 1940, the number had dropped to a combined ten, demonstrating how education and the work of their parents and grandparents to save money and start businesses helped the second and third generations to have more opportunities than their forebears.

However, even among the later generations, it is likely that many who had permanent jobs would take on additional work to earn anything they could. Seasonal work was a trend among Italians not only in Maine, but in other areas of the United States, as Italians were willing to do any work from ragpicking to berrypicking to get by and to support their families.[160] Mary Ann Ricci recalled that her father worked construction in the summer, and in the winter worked for the city in terrible conditions:

> Mary Ann: ... Dating my mother, I remember my dad telling me... this story where he's going to pick up my mother one Saturday afternoon in the winter, it was freezing, and my mother said, we'll go up to the dance or whatever, but first will you bring this thermos of hot coffee to my father, he's down at what is now Back Bay where they used to snowplow all the snow into the ocean.
>
> My father's take on that was, look, I don't play waterboy for anyone, I don't care who your father is, I don't care how much I have to impress him. So he reluctantly takes the thermos of coffee down. So he pulls in, I'm gonna cry while I say this, so he pulls into the parking lot and there's no window on the thing so his face is covered in ice and he said when he saw my father he smiled and the ice cracked on his face. That made such an impression on my dad, my dad was like, I'd walk a hundred miles to bring that man coffee.

> That was the job. That was the
> winter job. That was how you fed a family
> of eight. So he was down there plowing
> snow into the bay and my father said,
> when he saw him his face was just
> covered in ice and when he saw him the
> ice cracked and that was how it came off
> his face.[161]

Rose Valente remembered that her father did whatever he could around the neighborhood, in addition to employment he found through the Works Progress Administration and his work as a longshoreman, and though it was for extra income, that income was not always guaranteed. If people could not pay Mr. Valente would do it for free, or they would pay what they could.[162] Such an attitude toward helping the neighborhood people in need was a carryover of an attitude from Italy, as in the Mezzogiorno, poverty was considered "a common problem that everyone in the community shared."[163]

Poverty was clearly an issue in Little Italy, as children also had to find ways to earn money outside of a set job like delivering newspapers or working for their parents in their grocery store or restaurant. Ragpicking was one such source of income:

> Allan Neff: A lot of the buildings that are
> now the Old Port along Middle Street I
> remember as a little kid taking a little
> wheelbarrow around the neighborhood
> collecting newspapers and there was a
> guy down at one of those buildings on
> Middle Street. He'd buy metal, rags, and
> newspapers like a half a cent a pound for

rags and a quarter cent a pound for newspapers. Like a recycling center. Used to take a wheelbarrow - not a wheelbarrow - like a little red wagon around.

Joe Guidi: You know what they did before that, though? These little Jewish guys would come to your house and say 'rags!' 'rags!' and we'd steal our mother's dresses.[164]

Ragpickers offered the children of the neighborhood, and undoubtedly adults too, the opportunity to earn much-needed extra money, and emphasize the working-class nature of the neighborhood in which the Italian community settled.

The working-class Little Italy was also dotted with shops operated by Italians. Though manual labor and manufacturing were key modes of wage-earning for Italians in Portland, the population also opened and operated businesses. As with contracting companies, the shops were located in the neighborhood and employed family and neighbors. The physical shops also served as gathering places for the community members. Barbershops, tailor shops, shoe shops, and, most popularly, food-related businesses, opened up under the ownership of Italians and employed their family members and neighbors.

Rocco Clemente ran a tailor shop in the neighborhood for over three decades. With a shop at 106 India Street, in a two story building that he owned as early as 1924, Clemente was an early success story among the Italian immigrants. He started out living in a rented apartment at 39 Middle Street with his wife and two children, and was working as a tailor at this time.[165] The 39 Middle Street building that Clemente initially lived in, just around the corner from his tailor shop, was also home to the Italian Bank, the Banco Correspondente di Napoli. [166] As home to Rocco Clemente and his family, a fixture in the neighborhood for decades, as well as a bank that undoubtedly would have been a gathering place for Italians, this building served as physical evidence of the close ties Italians had to all aspects of the neighborhood.

The 39 Middle Street building was eventually torn down, and the property is now an empty lot and another example of the physical evidence of Portland's Little Italy and its close community disappearing.

Location of 39 Middle Street in 2013. Photo by Author.

Alfred DiFiore was another tailor in Little Italy. He arrived in the United States in 1910, and by 1920, he was working as a tailor and living with his family at 63 Fore

Street. Alfred continued working as a tailor in his shop at 278 Middle Street through at least the 1950s, and, in the family-centric trend of the Italians, the shop also employed his son Dominic.[167]

Barbershops owned by Italians also employed family members and neighbors, as well as served as gathering places for the neighborhood men. As in other cities in the United States, Italians in Portland became associated with the craft of barbering. The Italians in Portland contributed to this aspect of Italian life in America, just as their counterparts in Boston and New York City did. The number of barbershops with Italian names listed in the city directories for the early twentieth century were numerous, as were the census notations of those working as barbers. Italians were not only employed as barbers, but they were owners of barbershops and, as was true in other industries and trades, employed other Italians in their shops

In 1910 the brothers James, Gaetano, and Antonio Caiazzo were all barbers, with James and Gaetano running their own shops and Antonio, as the youngest of the three, worked for one or both of his brothers. The three also lived together at 2 Middle Street, again emphasizing just how close Italian families were. The Caiazzo men not only lived together, they worked in the same trade, employing one another when necessary, and doing so all in the confines of the Italian neighborhood. By 1920, James was still running a barbershop, Antonio had moved up to running his own, and Gaetano appeared to have moved out of the Little Italy neighborhood, but was still working as a barber at 126 Middle Street as late as 1925.[168]

Several of the barbershops that operated in Portland were housed in buildings owned by Italian-Americans, again demonstrating the deep connections between Italians in the community. Vincenzo Mascis (likely actually Macisso), a fruit dealer in the neighborhood, owned a few buildings, including one at 42 Deer Street that housed a barbershop.[169] Another Italian-owned building was 41 Middle Street in which the Paolino and Quattrucci Barbershop was located. The Paolino and Quattrucci Barbershop was a well-known as a gathering spot in the neighborhood. Joe Guidi and Allan Neff recalled that the barbershop at this location, in a building owned by Michael Valente, was also home to "the green door" - the location to which people could go to purchase alcohol, or to play cards, without encountering any legal trouble:

> Allan Neff: Oh, the card playing...in the backroom at the barber shop they had a lot of card playing. Uncle Ray [Ray Maiorino] used to go back there!
>
> Joe Guidi: No, the thing is, years ago, I'm talking back in the forties. That was where everybody got their booze on the weekend.
>
> AN: I didn't know much about that. I had heard rumors - I'd heard about the card playing.
>
> Jamie: So through the green door is where everybody got their booze?
>
> AN: Even the police used to go back there.
>
> JG: Oh, yeah, I wouldn't be surprised."[170]

Such establishments were not uncommon in immigrant neighborhoods at the time, and served as yet another location in which the community life of Little Italy flourished. [171]

Like barbershops, poolrooms were a popular gathering spot for Italian men, and the proliferation of them in the neighborhood in the 1925 Portland City Directory emphasizes this. Just as with barbershops, Little Italy was packed with poolrooms owned and staffed by Italians. Frank DiMeigo owned a poolroom at 41 ½ Middle Street, a building that also hosted the Paolino and Quattrucci Barbershop. By 1929 another Italian-owned poolroom had opened on the same block of Middle Street - Antonio Camlota's business at 47 Middle Street.[172] In 1925 several other poolrooms were operating in Little Italy.

The high concentration of businesses that served as community gathering spots shows the prominence that socializing with one another held for the men of the neighborhood, as well as the sheer Italian identity of the neighborhood. From the manual labor to working in shops, the one constant that remains throughout the years and across the various businesses and trades of Little Italy is that family members and neighbors often employed one another or worked side-by-side, and did so in the businesses, factories, and shops close to their homes in Little Italy. The people of Little Italy worked hard to survive, but family and community were always a key component of life, even contributing to the ability of certain businesses to start and to the overall survival of the people of the neighborhood.

RESTAURANTS AND GROCERY STORES

Food is one of the central cultural identifiers of Italians in the United States - both inside and outside the home. In the homes of Little Italy, the kitchen was the center of activity. It was where the families gathered and where the adults socialized, no matter in which Italian enclave one lived. Even in New York, with its vast opportunities for socialization compared to Portland, "If you took the kitchen table out of an Italian home that would be the end of any social life."[173] Food, and the family life that took place around it, was much more important for Italians than the mere act of eating.

The preparation, cooking, and eating of Italian food in the warm company of relatives and friends takes on a ritualistic significance among Italian-Americans, for it symbolizes the family's victory which accompanies that condition.[174]

Memories of food and its role in the home and community remain strong for those who grew up there. Allan Neff recalled how his grandmother, Joe Guidi's mother, was famous in the neighborhood for her pizza:

> One of the things that the neighbors really enjoyed was her pizza. She had a square pan that was exactly the same size as the inside of the oven and it was a deep pan and she would roll out her own...pizza dough, push that into the corners of the pan, smear it with olive oil, put her own special pizza sauce on there, along with about 5 pounds of meat, 5 pounds of cheese, cut up vegetables. Onions, green peppers, black olives, and about twenty minutes or so after she put that in oven we'd start getting knocks at the door. 'Josephine you're cooking pizza!' People were coming from blocks away, just grab'em by the nose and pull'em in. Oh, that pizza was to die for.[175]

Interestingly, pizza did not seem to have entered the Portland mainstream as late as 1940. The Portland City Guide for that year made a point of explaining what pizza is, demonstrating how the Italians were perhaps still on the edges of Portland society even 60 years after they began clustering in the neighborhood.

Mary Ann (Ricci) Butts recalled that the kitchen was the center of her family's house at 39 Hampshire Street, with relatives sitting on stairs and crowding in any way they could to be together for meals. She, her mother, and aunt also explained that what they served on holidays they did not consider to be a meal, but in other cultures the sheer amount of food would have been considered more than a meal. At the Sangillo household, Mrs. Sangillo made bread and pasta each day. On Sundays the Sangillo children who had married and left home brought their families to dinner at their parents' home.

In addition to food, homemade wine was an important aspect of life for Italian-Americans, as it provided a way to keep part of the old way of life with them in the United States. It remained prevalent among the first generation of immigrants even during the Prohibition era, and was an art in which the Italians took great pride.[176]

> Joe Guidi: My father, plus he made his wine. I don't care how bad things got he always made his wine.

> Allan Neff: In fact he had his daughters stomping the grapes in the wine cask.

> JG: You know why that happened, don't you? He used to use Grampie's...Grampie had the squasher, you know...I guess him and my father were in an argument so my father had to do it by hand. So all of us kids would take our shoes off, wash our feet, and squash the grapes.

> AN: I remember when he used to make his own wine. Even on Monument Street!

JG: Oh, all the time. Always made his wine. He always came up with money for those grapes. Always.[177]

Though the families of Little Italy did not have much money, and the people often worked extremely hard for what little they had, they found the money to carry on their culture through food and wine, both of which were also a reason for families to gather together. The Italians also used their strong connection to food to earn money, starting businesses that were based on selling food items to their Italian neighbors. The grocery and restaurant industries provided a way for Italian immigrants to make a living while nurturing their culture – not only food, but also close community through employment of family members and neighbors, with many businesses passed down through family members over generations.

Restaurants, groceries, bakeries, delis, and produce shops were prevalent in Portland's Little Italy, crowded in among the apartment buildings. As Rose Valente remembers: "I had to stay pretty close to home, sheltered... but there were so many grocery stores in the neighborhood. It seems as though every corner was a grocery store."[178]

With staples such as groceries accessible so close to home, even as late as the 1940s, the Italians of the neighborhood did not have to venture far from their neighborhood if they did not want to, and that certainly contributed to the strength of their community. With family members and friends from of the same ethnicity and speaking the same language as themselves, business owners had a built-in customer base in the ethnic enclaves that existed both in Portland and across the United States.[179] As a result, these businesses thrived and Portland's Italians were able to spread a piece of their culture to the wider population of Maine.

Amato's is an excellent example of how Portland's Italian-American population has influenced the culture of the state as a whole. As with many Italian businesses, it started as a family and community-centric Italian business, but Amato's now has locations throughout New England and as recently as 2002 the business was honored with the Governor's Award for Business Excellence.[180] In an interview about his experiences with the neighborhood, Michael Fixaris reminisced about how as late as the 1970s the India Street neighborhood was a spot where his family would make a point of going for specialty foods and to eat and socialize at restaurants, even though his own family was not of Italian-American descent.[181]

Amato's is an anchor for the Italian-American identity of the neighborhood as it is one of the earliest prominent Italian-American names in the city, with the original "Maine Italian" sandwich tracing its origins back to Giovanni Amato's sale of them to laborers as early as 1902. Made with a soft roll, cheese, ham, onions, tomatoes, green peppers, pickles, olives, and topped with salt, pepper, and olive oil, the sandwich is a treat still mostly known only in Maine. In this way, the Italian-Americans contributed to a unique facet of Maine's culture. Interestingly, the family history book for the Lorello, DeSarno, Villacci, Valente[182] family of Portland claims that it was a Lorello who invented the Italian Sandwich - in the Deering neighborhood of Portland.

However, the popular mythos of Portland follows the Amato's story, and as the Amato's would have been located in the heart of Little Italy and near the many Italians working on the waterfront, at Grand Trunk, and in other labor capacities, it is arguably a more likely story of the conception of the sandwich. That the Italian sandwich is such a hallmark of Portland's Italian-American community to have two (at least) families and businesses claiming its roots shows not only the sandwich's importance to the business community and wider Italian-American community, but also to the impact of both on Portland and Maine's wider culture.

Though it has become a large, successful business Amato's stayed rooted in its identity as a family business based in Portland's Little Italy. Rather than employ an outside, professional advertising model, Amato's used Teresa Ciampi in its ads. Mrs. Ciampi grew up in Little Italy, and her parents owned Commercial Fruit, which was an Italian grocery store. When Commercial Fruit closed in the 1970s, she began working down the street at Amato's, and "at some point, her photograph ended up on Amato's menus." Then, "Somehow, it went from there to the sides of buses in Portland," her son said."[183]

Even in the 21st century, Amato's remains rooted in Little Italy, as the Reali family, another family from the neighborhood, bought Amato's from the Amato family in the 1970s. Frank Reali still touts the business' story, emphasizing the role of Giovanni Amato's family, and the Italian working community in its success:

> "Frank Reali likes to tell the story of how Giovanni worked on road gangs, and his wife made him a daily sandwich of cold cuts and vegetables. The Italian sandwich was admired by all. The Amatos began delivering a few by horse and buggy. Soon

they were selling 1,000 a day to people lined up around the block."[184]

Giovanni's original shop was at 71 India Street, and there is still an Amato's at this location, though it has been enlarged and renovated.

The original building, with its awkwardly shaped front stairs, was razed in the late 1990s to make space for a patio area complete with a fountain, so that customers could enjoy their food outdoors on the corner of Newbury and India Streets.[185] The changing face of the original Amato's is indicative of how the neighborhood itself continues to change and to move away from its working class, immigrant history. However, though the physical environment of the neighborhood has changed the Italian culture still persists in some way.

Anania's Variety, a sandwich shop and convenience store, is no longer located in Portland's Little Italy, but is a prime example of the staying power of Portland's Italian businesses and of the family involvement in those businesses. The store was once known as the Newbury Street Market because of its location in Little Italy. Peter Anania was the patriarch of the family that started this store. Demonstrating the deep roots this store had in Little Italy, Peter Anania seems to have been somewhat of a legend in Little Italy, as a 1975 article on the neighborhood observes:

> We would like to pay special attention to Peter Anania, Sr. He is 91 years old, has all his hair, his teeth, has smoked cigarettes for years, a real cool character, he has now

switched to big, black cigars. He is a veteran of World War II who raised all his seven children when his wife died, when his kids were barely out of the toddling stage, and they are all doing great.[186]

In 1960 two of Peter's sons, Edward R. Anania and Joseph Anania were working at the Newbury Street Market, and lived with Peter at 47 Newbury Street.[187] Edward Anania, Jr., son of Edward R. Anania, is still active in running the Anania's stores today. Though originally located on Newbury Street, the Anania's stores moved off the peninsula to outer Congress Street in the Libbytown neighborhood of Portland. In the 1990s and early 2000s, Anania's expanded into East Deering with a Washington Avenue location, and then to South Portland with a Broadway location. The Washington Avenue location took over a store owned by another Italian family, the Pierobello family. Spearheaded by Constance 'Connie' Pierobello, that business was known as LaRosa's, which was Connie's maiden name. Anania's is a prime example of the importance of family to Portland's Italian community, and to the strength of the culture as such family and community ties persist today and help to keep stores that began in Portland's Italy decades ago to remain successful.

Micucci's is a vestige of the old Little Italy that, unlike Anania's, still stands in the neighborhood today. It was established long after the Amato's began baking bread and making sandwiches to sell to their fellow Italian-Americans. Located at 45 India Street, Micucci's was started in 1949 by Emilio (Leo) Micucci, and staffed in part by his son.[188] Micucci's came to prominence selling Italian foods and supplies that could not be found in Maine at the time, with Leo driving down to Boston to pick up the foods he sold. [189] The business is still owned and operated by the Micucci family and is still a destination for Italian families who want ingredients for specific dishes. Now, though, it is primarily a wholesale business that serves more than 200 restaurants and stores, and has expanded to include a variety of non-Italian food items, but does advertise that it specializes in pizza-making products.[190]

Micucci Grocery in 2013. Photo by Author.

Located on the opposite corner of Middle Street from Micucci's, at 47 India, Commercial Fruit was another Italian-owned family business in the neighborhood. Anthony and Frances (Atripaldi) Colello owned and ran the store, which was a prominent fixture in the neighborhood.[191] A branch of the family that ran the business included the face of Amato's - Teresa Ricci Ciampi, whose mother was an Atripaldi. She was deeply involved in the operation of the business. Though Mrs. Ciampi's father was a longshoreman he ended up helping in the store, as did Mrs. Ciampi and her son, Alex. "'We all worked there," Alex Ciampi said. "As a kid, I can remember putting soda bottles away. It was a blast. That's the place where I learned about family values, honesty and getting along with people." [192]Allan Neff, who is Italian on his mother's side, and who grew up in the neighborhood during the 1950s, recalled Commercial Fruit as the shop where his family purchased their groceries.

> And of course Commercial Fruit across the street there. I used to go do our grocery shopping there. You know, my mom and dad would give me a grocery list - things to go buy - that was at a time when they would keep a tab for you and you could buy on credit. They would just write down how much you owed and put it in the drawer and then dad would go over there when he got paid at the end of the week and pay the tab.[193]

Because of the closeness of the community, Italian families were able to trust one another enough to establish lines of credit at neighborhood stores. Though Commercial Fruit was certainly a neighborhood and family store while it operated from the 1950s to the 1970s, it also had a wider clientele than just the neighborhood Italians. "It became a gathering place for the Italian community, as well as politicians like former Maine Governors Joseph Brennan and James Longley. Several former professional wrestlers also frequented the store...Bruno Sammartino and Andre the Giant."[194] The site where Commercial Fruit once stood is now home to a hair salon and a realty company.

1940s Wedding Photo from Author's Family Collection. Commercial Fruit is in the back left, and Russo's Variety (later Al's Lunch, then Micucci's) is in the back right.

Like Commercial Fruit, the Village Café was a family-run business that grew to wider prominence in Portland, but the building that housed it has been demolished in the spate of development in the Little Italy neighborhood. Like Amato's, which a branch of the Reali family came to own, the Village Cafe initially catered to the workers of the waterfront neighborhood when Vincenzo and Maria Reali opened it on Newbury Street in 1936.[195] The business remained in operation until 2007, and over the course of those seven decades the restaurant expanded and became a major force in the neighborhood. Over the course of the seventy years it was in business the Village grew from a cafe with six stools and four booths[196] to a 500-seat family restaurant.[197]

In its early years, the Village was a family affair, as were many of the Italian businesses. Vincenzo ran the business, but Maria prepared the food. Vincenzo used a buzzer under the counter to let his wife know someone had ordered food. She would come from the family's apartment next door to cook the meal from the then-basic menu.[198]

At this time the Village Cafe, though it had food, was more of a bar, and served as yet another gathering place for the community.

> Jamie: What about the Village? Could you talk a little bit about that?
>
> Evelyn: We weren't allowed to go in there.
>
> Mary: It was a bar in the beginning. Well, there was a bar and a few booths there, but it was more a bar. They had pizza and you could sit and eat. I remember periodically I'd go over to get pizzas to take home.
>
> Evelyn: I don't remember, but I do know I wasn't allowed in.
>
> Mary: Because it was a bar then. But then they expanded and went into the big restaurant and had the bar up front.
>
> Evelyn: And then again you'd see kids running in and out, either because their families worked there, or their dads were in there having a drink before dinner. It was just a very safe place"[199]

Amedeo Reali, Vincenzo's son, eventually took over the business, with his children, Vincenzo's grandchildren, helping out. Michael Reali, in an interview with the Portland Press Herald recalled working in the restaurant when growing up: "My dad would have us snipping the ends of radishes to earn a hamburger."[200] Michael eventually left the family business, but did not lose his connection to the neighborhood as he relocated his insurance company in the late 1990s in an effort to help preserve Little Italy.

Like the Village Café, The Taliento Superette was a family business where people from the neighborhood would gather. It was located at the corner of Federal and Hampshire Street,[201] and was later known as the Federal Supermarket. The grocery store was started by Dominic Taliento. He was joined in working at the store by his brother, Michael, in 1930[202] and later the two of them were joined by their younger brothers Neil and Albert.[203] Albert later put his experience in the grocery store to use as a salesman for Prince Macaroni. He met his wife at this job, coincidentally in her family's grocery store.[204]

As with other businesses in Little Italy, the Talientos also hired neighborhood people to work alongside the family members. For example, Camilla Caiazzo Gorham, who grew up on Middle Street, worked there as a meat wrapper.[205] Like most businesses in Little Italy, the Taliento's store was not only a place people went to buy their groceries, but was also where people socialized. The Ricci sisters remembered how the kids in the neighborhood used to play around the store:

> Evelyn: The Talientos had the Federal Supermarket. Of course, every kid in the neighborhood was poor, we'd go up there

at night, they'd keep the pickles and different things outside in great big barrels, they had a barrel of snails, we'd go sneak the snails...We would sneak the snails and put them on the window (laughing) and bet whose was gonna reach the top. And then Mr. Taliento, his name was Coco, he let us get away with all kinds of stuff that today you wouldn't even dare do. God love him, if he had a big sale or something he'd come out and chase us away and his daughter Diane is right with us.[206]

From the children to the adults, the community life of Little Italy superseded all else, and is what remains clear in their memories of the neighborhood.

In a different vein from childhood gatherings at businesses in the neighborhood, is Sangillo's Tavern, which was and still is a gathering spot in Little Italy. Though Sangillo's did not exist in its current form during the heyday of Little Italy, it has existed in the neighborhood under the ownership of a Sangillo under various names and in various locations. Adam Sangillo, Sr. started the business as the Saco Grill in 1942. He then moved the business to two different India Street locations, the latter having to close in 1996 because of an expansion of Micucci's, from whom Sangillo rented the location. The bar then reopened on Hampshire Street.

Sangillo's Tavern, 2012. Photo by author.

Age eighty-three in 2000, Adam Sangillo was still tending bar and fostering the sense of community that is a part of what customers recognized as Sangillo's hallmark, to the extent that even customers who stopped drinking continued to go for a cup of coffee and conversation.

Adam's family was a fixture in Little Italy. He was born one of 26 children to Catarina and Frank Sangillo, 22 boys and 4 girls, and grew up on Freeman Lane in Little Italy.[207] In yet another example of business' started in Portland's Little Italy staying in the family, Adam's son, Adam, Jr., eventually took over the bar and managed it until his own death in 2008. Sangillo's remained open until it was shut down by the city of Portland in 2015.

Another family-run business in Little Italy was Cremo's Bakery, located at 8 Deer Street, in the heart of Little Italy. Unlike Sangillo's, Cremo's Bakery did not survive urban renewal in order to be passed down to new generations of the Cremo family. Owned by Michael (also known as Michele) [208] Cremo, it was located in the midst of apartment houses on Deer Street, within walking distance for all of Little Italy. Joe Guidi remembers going to Cremo's, and also remembers its closing.

> Very interesting story is Cremo's Bakery. Ever hear of that before? Best bread in the world. I'm glad they went out of business because I used to go down there and eat a loaf of bread. They gave Cremo $3,000 for his bakery and his building. To this day the check has never been cashed.[209]

Though Joe Guidi did not go into detail regarding the check not being cashed, the implication from the emotionally charged manner in which he told this story was that the bakery and building meant more to Mr. Cremo than any amount of money could make up for. Cremo's bakery was demolished as part of the urban renewal movement that took out all of Vine, Deer, and Chatham Streets. The 1945 Portland City Directory lists Michael Cremo as owning the bakery at 8 Deer Street, and also lists Michael and Josephine Cremo as residing at 10 Deer Street. Urban renewal destroyed both their home and business.[210] The destruction of the Cremo's Bakery building also took away the physical property with which Italians from the neighborhood associated happy memories: "Evelyn: ...And you'd go in, and you'd have to go down like four flights of stairs and he'd have two ovens. Oh, god that used to smell so good!"[211]

Al's Lunch was a family business in the strictest sense of the word, as Alphonso Russo and his wife Anna ran the restaurant, which was located merely a block from their home, and had previously been a store run by Anna's family - Cartonio's grocery. The restaurant played a large part in Anna's life, and that property is important to the overall interconnectedness of Portland's Italian community.

> Together they operated Al's Luncheonette at 45 India St. until 1964, when they sold the business to a neighborhood man who was hawking Italian items from the trunk of his car, said her son Joseph Russo. It would become Micucci's grocery.[212]

It was not unusual for Italian immigrant families to enter into the food service business, nor was it unusual for that food service business to be close to, or in, their residence and cater to neighbors and friends. Portland's Little Italy was rife with restaurants and grocery stores owned and staffed by the Italians of the neighborhood in which they were located. These businesses provided Italians with gathering places, a place to purchase ethnic foods, or any food, without venturing far from home and from a clerk who could understand them even if they did not speak English. With an Italian customer base, and eventually a larger swath of Portlanders as customers, businesses such as Amato's and Micucci's prospered. Not only were they able to employ more of their neighborhood brethren, but shared and continue to share Italian foods, and foods that originated in Portland's Little Italy, with all of Maine. Through their success, the Italian culture that emerged in Portland's Little Italy remains strong today, throughout the city and state.

Jamie Carter Logan

EDUCATION

Italian-Americans had a reputation for not placing an emphasis on the importance of education and of sending children to work at an early age: "As it was in Italy so it would be in the New World. Children were expected to hold jobs and contribute to the family income."[213] There are several theories as to why Italian immigrants did not send their children to school, above and beyond that of simply needing another full-time worker to contribute to the family income. One explanation is that Italian parents viewed the schools as "an inculcator of foreign values...," first and foremost would be that the children may lose sight of 'la famiglia' as their first priority.[214] As with other aspects of life in Little Italy, family trumped all else.

Italian children who were born in Maine, or who came to Maine at a young age did attend school, but many of those who emigrated as teenagers did not begin attending school in the United States, but rather helped out the family by working. The trend is evident through the 1920s, but records indicate that by 1930 more children of

Italian descent were attending school. By 1940 it becomes clear that most Italian children had surpassed or would surpass, their parents' educational accomplishments. The heads of households who were born in Maine were also far more likely than their counterparts born in Italy to have completed at least some high school. While there were some instances of Italian immigrants who had attended some high school it is rare, and eighth grade is a much more common upper level of academic achievement, though elementary levels were also common. By 1940, the children of Portland's Italian immigrants were beginning to move away from the sheltered Italian enclave and establish new patterns in education and work.[215] The change in education trends among Portland's Italians also shows the change taking place generationally, as later immigrants, or the children of immigrants, were more inclined to send their children to school and to see the value of education. However, children who attended school often worked as well, even from 1940 onward.

In the late nineteenth and early twentieth centuries there were a large number of Italian child workers due to the padrone system.[216] As the padrone system declined, however, the trend of children and teenagers working did not necessarily do the same. Families needed the income that their sons and daughters could bring in, and so the children would leave school and go to work full time; leaving school before they could prepare for a career beyond manual labor.

Portland's Little Italy has several examples of teenagers who left school to work. In 1920, sixteen year old Tony Salami lived on Vine Street with his brother, Joe, and widowed mother, Mary. The three of them arrived in the United States in 1911, and Tony did not attend school, though his thirteen year old brother did. At age sixteen Tony worked as a freight handler to support the family. [217]Antonette Trocci lived within a couple of blocks of the Salami family, at 38 India Street. Like Tony, she was only sixteen and did not attend school. Antonette, at age sixteen, was the only wage earner listed in this household of 11 people, employed as a waistmaker at the shirt factory. Undoubtedly, her other siblings and likely her father picked up some work where they could, but she appeared to be the only one with a steady job.[218]

James Berrino was also 16 in 1920, and instead of attending school was working with his father, also James, at the pipe factory.[219] James Berrino reflects the pattern of Italians who came to the United States in the earlier twentieth century, children who often did not attend American schools at all. James Berrino came to the United States in 1915 with his parents, James and Montalta. The family settled on Hampshire Street, and though James was only 11 at the time of immigration and their home was only blocks from both North School and Cathedral School, he did not attend school.

By 1930 the pattern changed somewhat and more Italian children were attending school. Furthermore, Italian parents could read, write, and speak English. However, literacy and English language fluency were certainly not universal in the neighborhood.

As more Italian children attended school, more were able to read and write. However, in the years leading up to 1930, when the trend starts to reverse toward Italian children attending school for at least some years, literacy rates remained low, especially among women. This fact aligns with the national data that shows "immigrant women were the largest group of illiterates."[220]

Italian women, unlike their Irish counterparts, came to the United States not only unable to speak English, but perhaps also speaking a distinct dialect of Italian that was unique to the region they came from, making it difficult to communicate with those from other regions or villages of Italy who lived in the neighborhood. The women who lived in Little Italy were less likely to work outside the home or neighborhood than their husbands, fathers, and sons, and, as a result, had far less exposure to the English language.

Rose Valente, whose parents made a point of emphasizing the importance of education, recalled that her own mother was unable to read and write.

> Jamie: ... she couldn't read or write in Italian or English?

> Rose: No. She never went to school. I can remember my father trying to teach her how to read, I mean how to write her name. Because she wasn't a citizen and she had to know how to sign her name.[221]

In 1917 a literacy requirement for entrance to the United States was included in the Immigration Act passed by Congress.[222] The added requirement did not have much effect on the Portland population by 1920, but by 1930 literacy among the Italians in Portland increased.

Italian immigrants maintained some aspects of the culture in their new country, such as the primacy of family, but language was not one that immigrants shared with their children. While their parents spoke Italian at home, and many also spoke it at work, the children of immigrants were encouraged to speak only English, as it was their parents' hope that this would help them to succeed in the United States. Though at the time the younger generation seemed to embrace speaking only English, now, looking back, they regret not learning the language of their parents and grandparents as they held on to other aspects of Italian culture.

For instance, Rose Valente's older brother urged her to speak English, but she regrets not speaking Italian:

> Rose: I remember at times when I was little growing up, and I remember my brother Ralph, Ralph he was my oldest brother, he would come in and say ' you're in America, speak English' but I often think that may not have been a good idea. I think it would have been better if we'd learned both languages. But at the time... I can understand that.[223]

Joe Guidi and Allan Neff's parents and grandparents had the same attitude, and Joe, like Rose, regrets losing the language:

> Jamie: Did a lot of people speak Italian in the neighborhood - did your parents speak Italian or was it mostly English?
>
> JG: Oh, no. To each other, but never to us kids. We actually lost our language because the Italian people when they came over here they wanted to be part of the American thing. So they always spoke English to the kids and Italian to themselves.

AN: His parents - my grandparents - would always speak Italian to themselves but insisted their kids speak English.

JG: I don't know if you know this or not, but your mother, when she went to the first grade couldn't speak English, only Italian. When she died, she couldn't speak two words of Italian. I think what these foreigners are doing now teaching their kids their language, I think it's a good idea.[224]

The fact that the Italian immigrants did not view their language as worth saving, but did put certain values, such as the primacy of family, even above the education of their children, again emphasizes just how essential the strength of the family was in Little Italy. As second and third generation Italians now regret losing the Italian language, it is also clear that those of Italian descent have a clear connection to their heritage – a connection perhaps made stronger by the close-knit, Italian community in which they grew up.

RELIGION

The southern Italian peasants who came to the United States were different from their Irish Catholic counterparts, and as a result encountered difficulties in assimilating easily into the American Catholic Church. The Catholicism of the southern Italians was "deeply personal" and is credited for how it "strengthened urban neighborhoods and family life."[225] Faith was a connection to Italy, a connection to a life left behind, but a part of life that could be carried on in a new home and with people who understood and shared one's customs, such as deep veneration of the saints.

The earliest record of an Italian family in Portland comes from the Cathedral of the Immaculate Conception's parish records in the early 1880s.[226] Though Italian families certainly went to Cathedral, St. Joseph's, and other parishes in Portland, particularly as they began intermarrying other ethnicities such as the Irish and moving to areas throughout the city, St. Peter's was and continues to be the Italian Catholic Parish. It is even identified as such in the 1940 City Guide,[227] and the 1951 Portland Street Directory.[228] St. Peter's as a centerpiece of the neighborhood's Italian-

American identity cannot be discounted.

Father Angelo Santangelo founded St. Peter's in 1911 in a stable on Federal Street. The Bishop blessed the church on December 22nd of that year.[229] The establishment of St. Peter's during the time period was part of a national trend of increases in Italian parishes. By the end of World War I, there were over 500 Italian churches in the United States.[230] Completed and dedicated in 1930[231], the current St. Peter's Church is located at 72 Federal Street, with the rectory next door. An Italian contractor of Portland, C. Galli and Sons, based in Little Italy, was hired to build the church, and the designing architect was Michael Mastrangelo, an Italian native who lived in the Boston area.[232] Italian families funded the $60,000 cost of building St. Peter's through pledges. The construction of the physical church was a venture deeply rooted in community effort. As late as 1945, the parish was still offering masses in both Italian and English. The1945 *Portland City Directory* notes that the English mass was for children and the Italian mass was for adults, demonstrating how the children and grandchildren of those who emigrated were assimilating into American life in some ways and doing so with the blessing of their elders and the Church.

In a parish so closely tied to the ethnicity of its worshippers, it is not surprising that the priests serving the population would be of that same ethnicity. The priests serving the parish began with Fr. Santangelo, who moved on in 1913. From there, Fr. James Cary served until Fr. Anthony Petillo arrived and served until 1925. Fr. Gerald Burke then filled in until another Italian priest arrived. [233] Monsignor Teresio Domingo arrived in the United States in 1904 and began serving St. Peter's in 1927, after moving from a New York parish.[234] During his time in Portland, Fr.

Domingo travelled across Maine ministering to Italian populations throughout the state.[235] He lived at the rectory in the working class neighborhood amidst his parishioners. By 1940 a second priest had joined Fr. Domingo in the rectory - Fr. Gallacio Palladino who came from Connecticut.

Joe Guidi and Allan Neff both remembered having Monsignor Domingo as their parish priest:

> Joe Guidi: I go back to Fr. Domingo, now Fr. Domingo was the type of priest once you went into that Church you did not get up and walk out.
>
> AN: Oh, he was a tough priest. I remember serving his masses. He required certain things that you had to do, and you know, as an altar boy if you didn't say Latin right. I still remember my Latin today a lot because of Monsignor." [236]

Father Domingo passed away in 1975, and the parish hall is now named for him.

Reverend Joseph Romani was a native of Italy who first came to St. Peter's in 1946 and was the parish pastor from 1967-1983. In 1997 Portland's Italian American community honored Romani by starting a scholarship fund in his name.[237] Fr. Romani was more than just the parish priest, he was a member of the neighborhood community, visiting families in their homes and becoming a part of the family traditions.[238]

Other priests have since served the parish, including

Father Lawrence Sabatino who attended the parish while growing up. Fr. Sabatino was born in Maine and grew up on Vine Street in the home owned by his Italian immigrant parents.[239] To this day, the parish priest retains a connection to the neighborhood - Father Michael Seavey is a descendant of the Menario family.[240] St. Peter's Church remains central to Italians in southern Maine. Such was the case with Teresa Mancini Preston who moved to Raymond later in her life, but St. Peter's remained so important to her that in her later years she travelled to Portland to attend Mass at the neighborhood church of her childhood. Additionally, in a demonstration of the impact that St. Peter's had on many Italians in Portland, it is a near ubiquitous trend of the Italian-Americans who passed away in the 1990s and 2000s to have their funerals at the church.

Today, St. Peter's Church is not only one of the remaining physical structures of Portland's Little Italy, but is an institution that helps to hold the community together. One such event that emphasizes Portland's Italian community's strength even now is the "boisterous" festival that is the celebration of the Feast of St. Rocco. Fr. Gerald Burke is credited as the event's founder, and St. Peter's continues to host the festival each August on the street outside the Church as it has for the better part of a century.[241] The bazaar captures a major defining aspect of Portland's Little Italy: "...it is the human element - the long tables full of neighbors eating pizza or the volunteers helping at games - that speaks to the unity within this parish,"[242] and in doing so demonstrates why the bazaar continues to be so successful and why Portland's Italian community continues to be close-knit.

Recalling memories of the festival, or the 'Italian bazaar,' as it is also referred to, brought looks of joy to those interviewed about Little Italy. In one case, an interview was arranged at the request of the interviewee so that it would coincide with a family's annual plans to attend the 2013 bazaar. With the exception of the turtle races, which are no longer, the scene describing the bazaar from the 1940 Portland City Guide is still remarkably accurate: "The Italians of Portland, in conjunction with the Feast of the Assumption...turtle race, greased pole, parade, street fair at St. Peter's, and the making of pizza..."[243]

The greasy pole is still the center of the bazaar's activities (if one does not consider the food booths as activities) as attendees gather around to watch as young people try to reach the top of the pole to get the monetary prize. In the early days of the bazaar, meats and cheeses were hung from the top of the pole and were a valuable prize to be shared with the winners' families.[244]

The Greasy Pole at the 2013 Bazaar. Photo by Author.

In addition to eating, catching up with old friends and extended family, and cheering on the greasy pole contenders, many people still gather around the low-priced games, including ones created and set up each year by the parish such as the muffin tin game, which again shows the continuity of the traditions at the bazaar, as it would be very easy to abandon these hand-painted muffin tins and have only purchased dime-toss game setups.

> Mary Ann: I lived around the corner so my whole family would come up. Again, there'd be twenty people upstairs all smoking in that giant room. And my aunts would save change, they'd save change in this giant change purse and my aunt Helen and my Aunt Mary would totally flush us out with coins to play these toss games. And then there was this game that all I remember is all Italian men would be around it. Now when you come there's younger people involved, but when I was little it was all old Italian men and it was this game where they'd put muffin tins. Like fifteen muffin tins and they colored each one of the muffin tins, so there was red, yellow, green, blue, black, whatever, and then all around it was four 2x4s painted up and you'd put money on the circle to bet and it would pay off 2 to 1, 3 to 1, 4 to 1, whatever and I just remember then they'd let this ball go and wherever the ball landed, whatever muffin tin, that was the one that won. The giant roar that would come up on it, you know...[245]

Of the kids who attend the bazaar today, many are playing the same games their parents, grandparents, and even great-grandparents played, though they are likely traveling farther to do so.

A description of an Italian religious festival in New York City's Little Italy is remarkably similar to St. Peter's bazaar, except perhaps in the size of the celebration, including the procession of saints. The procession of saints still begins the St. Peter's Bazaar, with statues of saints displayed for the duration of the festival and, in the Italian tradition, people pinning money on them as an offering.

Offerings to Saints at 2012 St. Peter's Bazaar. Photo by Author.

The preparations for the festival take six months, and require help from several generations of parishioners preparing food and managing booths. In the days leading up to the festival over 7,000 Italian cookies are made by parishioners, including many who have been involved for decades, and whose families have been involved for generations. The parishioners make the cookies using ingredients from Micucci's grocery store and bake them right in the parish hall. The large pizza ovens in the parish hall underscore the central role the bazaar plays in parish life, as well as the central role food plays in Italian culture overall.[246]

A relatively recent addition to the bazaar festivities is the St. Peter's 4-miler Road Race, held on the Friday evening of the festival weekend. The idea for this addition to the festivities came from Joe Discatio[247], a prominent member of Portland's Italian community who owned Joe's Smoke Shop on Congress Street. Discatio grew up in Little Italy, the oldest of six children born to Italian immigrants, and had close ties to St. Peter's Church throughout his life. His 2012 obituary states:

> St. Peter's Catholic Church in Portland also held a very special place in his heart. Joe was very active in planning the annual bazaar as well as their annual road race. Many years ago, Joe was also the organizer of their annual variety shows. He was also a long time member of St. Peter's Holy Name Society.[248]

For over a century, St. Peter's Church has been a dominant factor in the lives of Portland's Italians. Members of the community built the church, served as its priests, and continue to attend Mass there even though the Little Italy in which they once lived is long gone. St. Peter's Church, and its annual St. Rocco Festival, are certainly most closely associated with Roman Catholicism currently, but other denominations in Portland served Italians during the heyday of Little Italy. The Italian Methodist Episcopal Church, "constituted a rival in the Italian community to St. Peter's Catholic Church that was located not too far from it on the same street"[249] and the Italian Pentecostals "met in a building around the corner from St. Peter's Church on Federal Street."[250]

Across the United States, the Methodist Church was invested in an outreach effort to Italians, a concerted effort to prove that Italians could be assimilated into American culture and to overcome what the Methodists saw as the Catholic Church's oppression of Italians.[251] With the foundation of the Italian Methodist Episcopal Church in the midst of the Italian enclave on Federal Street, it is clear that the Methodist Church recognized Portland as a city in which there was an Italian community large enough to be in need of a Methodist Church. The church also established a social meeting place for Italians on the upper floor of its pastor's residence.[252] Here, again, is evidence of how important gathering together community members was to Italians.

The 1930 and 1940 censuses show a Thomas/Tomasso Caliandro, a Pastor, living with his family at 130 Federal Street - merely down the block from St. Peter's Church. The 1930 census lists him as a Methodist pastor who arrived in the United States from Italy in 1924.[253] By 1940 he and his wife, Francisca, also an Italian immigrant, were raising their two children on Federal Street.[254] Like St. Peter's, the Italian Methodist Church had extremely strong links to Italy and the Italian culture, and as a result would have helped to keep the Italian identity of the Portland's Italian community strong.

As with work, grocery shopping, and socializing, the Italians of Portland did not have to leave their neighborhood to attend church. Whether they attended the Catholic Church or the Methodist Church, the Italian community of Portland was still among their family and neighbors and in a setting in which their culture was understood. The churches certainly helped to strengthen the community during the early years of the Italian settlement in Portland, and have continued to serve as a place for the Italian culture and the close-knit community of Portland to be preserved and celebrated.

DECLINE OF THE NEIGHBORHOOD

In the 1950s, Portland's Little Italy - specifically the Vine, Deer, and Chatham street areas - came under scrutiny for the conditions of the buildings and the crowdedness of the neighborhood. Following the creation of the Slum Clearance and Redevelopment Authority of Portland (SCRAP), the 6.3 acres of Vine-Deer-Chatham were deemed to be a slum. However, as with New York's Little Italy, the houses were so much more than what they appeared to be to the deciding authorities in Portland: "But Vine-Deer-Chatham was home to 62 families. It was a neighborhood with strong ethnic feeling. Many residents were Italian-Americans and it had been their home since they crossed the Atlantic decades earlier."[255]

The authorities of Portland did not see this community, though. They did not see how the neighborhood served as a home away from home for so many immigrants - some of whom still did not speak English - and who had created the enclave as a way to stay close to their family and fellow villagers in the United States. Crowded quarters were not necessarily a problem for the Italians of Portland, nor was living in an apartment directly above a store - which they or they children or cousins might own, or in which they or their family members worked. Instead, the neighborhood was viewed as "a seedy waterfront industrial and residential area located around India Street."[256]

This work seeks to add a different perspective to that understanding of the neighborhood by chronicling the sense of this community and the foundations of family on which it was built. The resilience of Portland's Italian community today is due to the family ties that served as its foundation. The neighborhood has now changed beyond just the physical environment, and has become a tourist destination and a neighborhood geared toward younger professionals, not working-class families. Since 1957 and the destruction of Vine-Deer-Chatham, the neighborhood has moved steadily away not only from its Italian identity, but from its working-class identity and identity as a starting place for new immigrant communities in Portland. From George Cleeve in the 17th Century right up through the 1950s the neighborhood served as a community for immigrants.

Now, it is not a community, but a landing place for tourists. A Hampton Inn, a Marriot Residence Inn, parking garages, upscale and 'hipster' restaurants line the streets where there once were groceries and poolrooms and barbershops established and patronized by those who lived, attended school, and went to church, within blocks of them. Urban renewal and subsequent construction have done more than change the landscape: "...the bulldozers and wrecking balls cleared away more than dilapidated buildings; they eviscerated communities, memories, and the sense of place..."[257] Perhaps most obviously poignant, is the site of the Village Café. Once a restaurant that catered to working-class men and then their families it is now a construction site for luxury condos.

The Former Site of the Village Café in 2013. Photo by Author.

As writer Colin Woodard observes, "Most of the development here is being built from scratch in a part of town whose rich past has been largely destroyed by war, fire, economic catastrophe, and wrongheaded urban "renewal" projects. New construction reflects this historical amnesia, producing a new "neighborhood" not unlike any other gentrified, urban tourist district in the country."[258] As the physical evidence of the neighborhood and its close-knit community are lost, an effort must be made to preserve the memory of that culture that perpetrated that community, and in doing so, provided a base for themselves to start a life in the United States from which their families grew and have provided so much to Portland. From the birds of passage who first came and lived in the neighborhood as boarders, to the family members they brought over, to the families created through marriage, the neighborhood provided the location in which immigrants could find work nearby and benefit from being around people who understood their culture as they did what they could to move upwards in American society. Though it perhaps took the Italians a bit longer than it had taken other ethnic groups to do so because of the language barrier and attitudes toward education, not to mention the abject poverty from which they were fleeing, the Little Italy of Portland provided a base for families to thrive in the United States.

Though the neighborhood itself has steadily lost its Italian identity, and the physical destruction of Portland's Little Italy that began during the urban renewal process of 1957 continues through the twenty-first century, the Italian community in Portland remains strong. The Italian Heritage Center is still active, and St. Peter's Church and its associated bazaar remain popular. Sandwich shops, businesses, and restaurants bearing Portland's 'old Italian names' still dot the city and keep Portlanders at least peripherally aware of the Italian community's influence on present day Portland, and even Maine. What has been lost, aside from what is passed down as family stories, is the day to day life and cultural history of the Italians of Portland and the neighborhood that was at the center of their lives. The neighborhood was created and kept strong through the connections and cooperation of family members, and those family connections provided the strength for the survival of Little Italy and the survival of Portland's Italian community even after Little Italy's physical environment was destroyed.

ABOUT THE AUTHOR

Jamie Carter Logan was born and raised in Portland, Maine. A graduate of Deering High School, the Catholic University of America, and the University of Maine she now works and resides in Augusta where she lives with her husband Bill and cat, Rosalita.

BIBLIOGRAPHY

"1924 City of Portland Tax Records." Maine Memory Network, Maine's Online History Museum, a Project of the Maine Historical Society. Accessed July 2011-April 2014. Http://www.mainememory.net/.

"About Pine State Trading Co." About Pine State Trading Co. Accessed March 20, 2014. http://www.pinestatetrading.com/AboutUs/tabid/70/Default.aspx.

"About Us The Nappi Legend." About. Accessed March 20, 2014. http://nappidistributors.com/about_us/default.aspx.

"AGC Maine Presidents." Associated General Contractors of Maine. Accessed March 20, 2014. Http://agcmaine.org/about/leadership-committee-chairs/agcmainepresidents/.

"Albert J. Fasulo, 78." *Portland Press Herald*, August 11, 2000. Accessed August 28, 2013.

"The Amato's Bakery." Amato's - Pizza :: Pasta :: Sandwiches - The Amato's Bakery. Accessed January 10, 2014. http://www.amatos.com/bakery/.

Amoruso, Marino. *Being Italian: A Memoir*. Bohemia, NY: Bailey Park Publishers, 2012.

"Ann C. Guimond Kitchen Supervisor for 22 Years." *Portland Press Herald*, April 24, 1999. Accessed December 31, 2013.

"Anna C. Decarolis Communicant of St. Peter's Church." *Portland Press Herald*, November 28, 1995. Accessed January 06, 2014.

"Anthony Carmine Fornisano." *Portland Press Herald*, June 12, 2012. Accessed December 30, 2013.

"Anthony Galli Self-employed Mason Contractor." *Portland Press Herald*, January 28, 1999. Accessed December 31, 2013.

"Antonio Bifulco Obituary." *Portland Press Herald*, August 28, 2013.

"Antonio G. Anania, 79." *Portland Press Herald*, June 05, 2000. Accessed January 06, 2014.

Aull, Elbert. "Delia A. Dalfonso, 87, Beautician and Devoted Grandmother." *Portland Press Herald*, March 11, 2008. Accessed December 31, 2013.

Banfield, Albert T. "The Padrone, the Sojourners, and the Settlers: A Preface to the 'Little Italies' of Maine." *Maine Historical Society Quarterly* 31, no. 3&4 (Winter 1992): 114-41.

Bartlett, Will. "All Four Mazziottis Are Still Together, Even after 50 Years." *Portland Press Herald*, June 22, 1996.

_____. "Anna Vacchiano Volunteer for Children's Cancer Fund." *Portland Press Herald*, December 07, 1995. Accessed December 30, 2013.

_____. "Armand 'al' Reali Musician-band Leader, Mmc Barber." *Portland Press Herald*, December 22, 1995. Accessed December 31, 2013.

_____. "Carmine `tom' Piscopo Bakery Route Driver, Golfer." *Portland Press Herald*, September 03, 1997. Accessed December 30, 2013.

_____. "Dominic Candelmo Shoe and Hat Repairer, Native of Italy." *Portland Press Herald*, November 21, 1996. Accessed December 30, 2013.

_____. "Liliana Donatelli Businesswoman, Lifelong Learner." *Portland Press Herald*, January 07, 1999. Accessed December 31, 2013.

_____. "Mary Josephine Mancini Owned Portland Tavern; Jay Leno Fan." *Portland Press Herald*, May 20, 1999. Accessed January 06, 2014.

Bauman, John F. *Gateway to Vacationland: The Making of Portland, Maine*. Amherst: University of Massachusetts Press, 2012.

"Bernadino Guidi Merchant Mariner, Businessman." *Portland Press Herald*, May 29, 1997. Accessed December 30, 2013.

http://libraries.maine.edu.ursus-proxy-11.ursus.maine.edu/mainedatabases/authmaine.asp?url=http://search.proquest.com.ursus-proxy-11.ursus.maine.edu/docview/276787062?accountid=17222.

Blom, Eric. "At Home in LITTLE ITALY Sangillo's Tavern Reopens a Block from Its Old Spot -- with the Same Air of Easy-going Banter." *Portland Press Herald*, February 19, 2000. Accessed December 30, 2013.

Bouchard, Kelley. "Backed by Demand ; The Germanis Un-retire to Run Corsetti's Restaurant Again in Portland." *Portland Press Herald*, March 18, 2004. Accessed January 06, 2014.

_____. "Cafe Going, Condos Coming An 82-unit Building Will Replace the Landmark Restaurant." *Portland Press Herald*, June 03, 2008. Accessed December 2013.

_____. "Theresa Mancini Preston, 72, Tenacious Mother, Student, Communicant." *Portland Press Herald*, May 12, 2003. Accessed December 31, 2013.

_____. "Village Cafe Seeks Buyer, New Location ; Owner John Reali Puts the Newbury Street Property on the Market as Interest in the Neighborhood Heats Up." *Portland Press Herald*, February 18, 2005.

Bouthillette, Emma. "Amedeo Reali, 83, Village Cafe Owner, Devoted to Family." *Portland Press Herald*, July 24, 2010. Accessed August 28, 2013.

_____. "Rose DeRice, 93, Hard-working, 'do-it-yourself' Mom." *Portland Press Herald*, October 06, 2010. Accessed December 31, 2013.

Bradbury, Dieter. "REDEFINING AMERICA IMMIGRANTS BROUGHT WITH THEM THE SEEDS OF AMERICA'S RICH AND DIVERSE SOCIAL FABRIC, BUT THEY ALSO WERE A THREAT TO THOSE WHO CAME BEFORE THEM. Series: Reader Roundtable." *Portland Press Herald*, October 15, 1995. Accessed December 2013.

Byrne, Matt. "Anna E. Russo of Portland Dies at Age 83." *Portland*

Press Herald, October 14, 2013. Accessed October 14, 2013.

"Camilla A. Gorham Foster Grandmother." *Portland Press Herald*, June 07, 1996. Accessed December 30, 2013.

"Camilla J. Olore." MaineRemembers.com - Camilla J. Olore. April 21, 2008. Accessed February 5, 2014..

"Camillo A. Giusti Longshoreman, Army Veteran." *Portland Press Herald*, March 10, 1998. Accessed January 6, 2014.

"Carmine J. Sonny Rumo." *Portland Press Herald*, August 21, 2013. Accessed August 21, 2013.

Carnevale, Nancy C. *A New Language, a New World: Italian Immigrants in the United States, 1890-1945*. Urbana: University of Illinois Press, 2009.

Ciongoli, A. Kenneth., and Jay Parini. *Beyond The Godfather: Italian American Writers on the Real Italian American Experience*. Hanover, NH: University Press of New England, 1997.

Conforti, Joseph A. *Creating Portland: History and Place in Northern New England*. Hanover, NH: University Press of New England, 2005.

Connell, William J., and Fred L. Gardaphé. *Anti-Italianism: Essays on a Prejudice*. New York, NY: Palgrave Macmillan, 2010.

Connolly, Michael C. *Seated by the Sea: The Maritime History of Portland, Maine, and Its Irish Longshoremen*. Gainesville: University Press of Florida, 2010.

_____. *They Change Their Sky: The Irish in Maine*. Orono, Me.: University of Maine Press, 2004.

"Constance Pierobello." *Portland Press Herald*, December 17, 2012. Accessed December 31, 2013.

Creamer, Melanie. "Feature Obituary: Daniel Lorello, 87, Salesman Who Loved Family, Golf." *Portland Press Herald*, February 22, 2013. Accessed March 30, 2013.

_____. "Feature Obituary: Ralph J. Salamone, 88, Retired Water District Foreman." *Portland Press Herald*, June 25, 2013. Accessed August 08, 2013.

Creamer, Melanie. "Rocco Gedaro, 87, WWII Vet, Mail Carrier, Community Volunteer." *Portland Press Herald*, September 24, 2011. Accessed December 30, 2013.

Daniello, Gabrielle. "Ghost Street: The Restless World of Portland's India Street in the Early Twentieth Century." Thesis, University of Southern Maine, 2007.

Daniels, Roger. *Coming to America: A History of Immigration and Ethnicity in American Life*. New York, NY: HarperCollins, 1990.

DeSalvo, Louise A. *Crazy in the Kitchen: Food, Feuds, and Forgiveness in an Italian American Family*. New York: Bloomsbury, 2004.

"Diana M. Ferrante." *Portland Press Herald*, May 5, 2013. Accessed August 28, 2013.

"Dorothy Antonia Cavallaro Loving Mother, Grandmother." *Portland Press Herald*, January 25, 1996. Accessed December 31, 2013.

Evans, David. "Regenerating the Italian Race: The Italian Methodist Mission and the Americanization of Italian History." *Methodist History* 49, no. 3 (April 2011): 132-47.

"Feature Obituary: Theresa Ciampi, 78, Featured in Ad for Amato's." Portland Press Herald. Accessed March 06, 2013.

Fleming, Deirdre. "Italian Festival Tribute to Neighbors, Roots." *Portland Press Herald*, August 16, 2009. Accessed December 31, 2013.

Garber, Andrew. "Joseph Nunzi Germani Loving Husband and Father." *Portland Press Herald*, August 17, 1997. Accessed January 06, 2014.

Gesualdi, Louis J. *The Italian/American Experience: A Collection of Writings*. Lanham, MD: University Press of America, 2012.

"Giovanni Corsetti, 74." *Portland Press Herald*, May 06, 2001. Accessed January 06, 2014.

Gleason, Anne. "Ben Alfiero, 80; Son of Immigrants Started Harbor Fish Market." *Portland Press Herald*, April 12, 2008. Accessed December 30, 2013.

Goad, Meredith. "For Portland's Italians, A Cookie Bonanza." *Portland Press Herald*, August 8, 2013. Accessed August 8, 2013.

Greater Portland 350th Anniversary Publication: Portland's Past, Present & Future. Portland, Me.: Material World Pub., 1982.

"Guy J. Germani Bricklayer, Sports Enthusiast." *Portland Press Herald*, June 23, 1998. Accessed January 06, 2014.

"Hod." Merriam-Webster. Accessed April 02, 2014. http://www.merriam-webster.com/dictionary/hod.

Hoey, Dennis. "DiPietro's, 69-year-old Portland Sandwich Shop, Closing Its Doors." *Portland Press Herald*, August 09, 2013. Accessed December 2013.

_____. "Nunzi D'Alfonso, 79, Well-known Portland Contractor." *Portland Press Herald*, January 23, 2012. Accessed December 31, 2013.

Iorizzo, Luciano J., and Salvatore Mondello. *The Italian-Americans*. New York: Twayne Publishers, 1971.

"James A. Maiorano Life Member of Knights of Columbus." *Portland Press Herald*, March 10, 1998. Accessed December 30, 2013.

"James C. Lapomarda Communicant of St. Peter's Catholic Church." *Portland Press Herald*, January 06, 1999. Accessed December 31, 2013.

"John A. Profenno a Founder of Italian Heritage Center." *Portland Press Herald*, April 02, 1999. Accessed December 31, 2013.

"John C. D'Alfonso Retired from Family Construction Business." *Portland Press Herald*, October 14, 1999. Accessed April 6, 2014.

"Joseph L. Discatio." Portland Press Herald/Maine Sunday Telegram. Accessed December 30, 2013.

"Joseph Pallotta, 78." *Portland Press Herald*, May 14, 2011. Accessed February 15, 2011.

"Josephine Polito Urbano, 89." *Portland Press Herald*, January 20, 2000. Accessed January 6, 2014.

Kessner, Thomas. *The Golden Door: Italian and Jewish Immigrant Mobility in New York City, 1880-1915*. New York: Oxford University Press, 1977.

Kraut, Alan M. *The Huddled Masses: The Immigrant in American Society, 1880-1921*. Arlington Heights, IL: Harlan Davidson, 1982.

Lacognata, A.A. "We The Italians of Maine." University of Maine at Portland-Gorham. Spring 1975.

Lapomarda, Vincent A. *A History of the Italians in the State of Maine*. Lewiston: Edwin Mellen Press, 2010.

Lau, Edie. "Alfred C. Ciampi Brick and Stone Mason." *Portland Press Herald*, May 12, 1996. Accessed January 06, 2014.

Lorello, DeSarno, Valente, Villacci Family History Book.

"Lucia Donatelli DiPietro Jarred Vegetables, Fruits of Her Own Garden." *Portland Press Herald*, December 02, 1999. Accessed December 31, 2013.

"Lucia "Lucy" Pastore, 93." *Portland Press Herald*, January 23, 2001. Accessed December 30, 2013.

Lunt, Dean. "GIVING BACK TO THE NEIGHBORHOOD A Growing Insurance Agency Saves a Piece of Portland History While Finding a New Downtown Location." *Portland Press Herald*, October 26, 1999.

Mangione, Jerre, and Ben Morreale. *La Storia: Five Centuries of the Italian American Experience*. New York: HarperCollins Publishers, 1992.

"Margaret Napolitano, 94." *Portland Press Herald*, October 12, 2000. Accessed December 30, 2013.

"Mary Fasulo Obituary." *Portland Press Herald*, March 19, 2013. Accessed January 06, 2014.

"Mary Germani Breault Obituary." Concord Monitor. Accessed December 30, 2013.

McNally, Jake. "Tearing the Heart Out of LIttle Italy." Munjoy Hill Observer. Accessed January 05, 2014.

"Michelina Feeney Communicant of St. Peter's." *Portland Press Herald*, June 08, 1998. Accessed December 31, 2013.

Mulkern, John. "Old St. Peter's Parish: Early Italian Families Settling in Portland." *The Wise Guide* (Portland, ME), July 18, 1975, Neighborhoods sec.

"'The Passing of an Era': Landmark Portland Italian Sandwich Shop Closes after 69 Years." *Bangor Daily News*, August 20, 2013. Accessed August 20, 2013.

Payne, Nancy, ed. *Greater Portland Community Guide*. Portland, Me.: Tower Pub., 1970.

"Philip A. Maietta, 88." *Portland Press Herald*, March 25, 2007. Accessed December 31, 2013.

"Philip Thomas Lombardi." *Portland Press Herald*, April 13, 2013. Accessed August 28, 2013.

Polito, Nancy Jo. *"Nobody Washes Me, I'm Italian!": From Italy to America, the Life Story of Armando Polito... His Way*. Denver, CO: Outskirts Press, 2011.

Portland City Directory. Portland, Me.: Tower Publishing, various years.

Portland City Guide. Portland: Forest City Print., 1940.

"Portland Maine History 1786 to Present | Facebook." Facebook. Accessed January 2012-April 2014.

Portland, South Portland, Cape Elizabeth Directory of Streets and Information. Portland, Me.: Interstate Pub., 1951.

Price, H. H., and Gerald E. Talbot. *Maine's Visible Black History: The First Chronicle of Its People*. Gardiner, Me.: Tilbury House, 2006.

Puleo, Stephen. *The Boston Italians: A Story of Pride, Perseverance, and Paesani, from the Years of the Great Immigration to the Present Day*. Boston: Beacon Press, 2007.

Rolfe, John. "St. Peter's 4-miler Has a Rich History, Some of It Serious." *Portland Press Herald*, July 20, 1997. Accessed December 31, 2013.

"Rosa Floridino Worked at Amato's, Village Cafe." *Portland Press Herald*, December 01, 1995. Accessed January 06, 2014.

Solloway, Steve. "Three Football Generations, with Nary a Gap in Talent." *Portland Press Herald*, September 01, 2002. Accessed December 30, 2013.

"St. Peter's to Honor Romani with Scholarship." *Portland Press Herald*, October 11, 1997. Accessed December 31, 2013.

Staff Reports. "Landmark Village Cafe Set to Close Saturday." *Portland Press Herald*, November 27, 2007. Accessed December 30, 2013.

"Stefanina E. Germani Remembered as Devoted to Her Family." *Portland Press Herald*, March 29, 1998. Accessed December 30, 2013.

"Thomas A. Valente Sr., 82." *Portland Press Herald*, February 02, 2000. Accessed December 30, 2013.

Tice, Lindsay. "Emmanuele Cobisi Laborer, Native of Sicily; Loved to Cook." *Portland Press Herald*, November 17, 1999.

"Twentieth Century Statistics." United States Census. Accessed February 20, 2014. http://www.census.gov/prod/99pubs/99statab/sec31.pdf.

United States. Census Bureau. *1910 US Census*. Accessed May/June 2013. http://www.ancestry.com/.

United States. Census Bureau. *1920 US Census*. Accessed July/August 2013. http://www.ancestry.com/.

United States. Census Bureau. *1930 US Census*. Accessed January/February 2014. http://www.ancestry.com/.

United States. Census Bureau. *1940 US Census*. Accessed March 2014. http://www.ancestry.com/.

Vegh, Steven G. "Community Policing Seems to Limit Gangs Foot and Bike Patrols in the West End and Little Italy Reassure Residents." *Portland Press Herald*, August 13, 1996. Accessed December 30, 2013.

_____ G. "An Italian (sandwich) Original to Be Torn down The Birthplace of Amato's Culinary Innovation Is No Oil Painting, Preservationists Agree." *Portland Press Herald*, December 13, 1999. Accessed December 30, 2013.

Violette, Zachary J. "The Aesthetics of Class and Ethnicity in the Renewal of Portland's Vine-Deer-Chatham Neighborhood 1920-1960." Thesis, University of Southern Maine, 2004.

Weinstein, Joshua L. "Donata Breggia, 110, Never Lost Attachment to Her Native Italy." *Portland Press Herald*, January 29, 2002. Accessed January 06, 2014.

Whyte, William Foote. *Street Corner Society: The Social Structure of an Italian Slum*. Chicago, IL: University of Chicago Press, 1955.

Willis, William. *The History of Portland. A Facsimile of the 1865 Ed.* Somersworth: New Hampshire Pub., 1972.

Woodard, Colin. "Portland's Forgotten Heart." The Bollard. Accessed March 30, 2014. http://thebollard.com/2007/12/06/portlands-forgotten-heart/.

Zimet, Abbie. "Albert J. Taliento, 78; Hard Worker, Had 'giant Heart'" *Portland Press Herald*, August 12, 2000. Accessed December 31, 2013.

_____. "City Life: Diversity Revitalizes Area Little Italy Reborn." *Portland Press Herald*, April 01, 1996. Accessed December 30, 2013.

_____. "Men 'who Never Came Home' Haunt Holiday Parade Leader for Nick Sangillo, a Veteran of the Normandy Invasion, Memorial Day Means Recalling the Pain of War and the Price of Freedom." *Portland Press Herald*, May 26, 1996. Accessed April 6, 2014.

Endnotes

[1] Mary Ricci, Evelyn Ricci, and Mary Ann (Ricci) Butts, interview by author, August 10, 2013.

[2] "1924 City of Portland Tax Records." Maine Memory Network, Maine's Online History Museum, a Project of the Maine Historical Society. Accessed July 2011-April 2014.

[3] Ibid.

[4] Kelley Bouchard, "Theresa Mancini Preston, 72, Tenacious Mother, Student, Communicant," *Portland Press Herald*, May 12, 2003, accessed December 31, 2013,

[5] *Portland City Guide* (Portland: Forest City Print., 1940), 60.

[6] Violette, "Portland's Vine-Deer-Chatham Neighborhood 1920-1960," 35.

[8] Puleo, *The Boston Italians*, xii.

[9] Iorizzo and Mondello, *The Italian-Americans*, 68.

[10] Lapomarda, *Italians in Maine*, 203.

[11] Ibid., pg. 203.

[12] Violette, "Renewal of Portland's Vine-Deer-Chatham Neighborhood."

[13] *Portland City Guide*, 60.

[14] Abby Zimet, "City Life: Diversity Revitalizes Area Little Italy Reborn," *Portland Press Herald*, April 01, 1996, accessed December 30, 2013,

[15] Kraut, *The Huddled Masses*, 80.

[16] Violette, *Vine-Deer-Chatham 1920-1960*, 28.

[17] Ibid., 9.

[18] Roger Daniels, *Coming to America,* 195.

[19] Mangione and Morreale, *La Storia,* 32-33.

[20] Ibid., 74.

[21] Connell and Gardaphé, *Anti-Italianism,* 23.

[22] Amoruso, *Being Italian,* 29.

[23] Connell and Gardaphé, *Anti-Italianism,* 120.

[24] *1940 Portland City Guide.*

[25] Michael Fixaris, interview by author, July 06, 2013.

[26] Mangione and Morreale, *La Storia,* 390.

[27] Ricci Family Interview

[28] Daniello, *Ghost Street,* 24.

[29] Dieter Bradbury, "Redefining America: Immigrants Brought With Them The Seeds of America's Rich And Diverse Social Fabric, but They Also Were a Threat to Those Who Came Before Them. Series: Reader Roundtable," *Portland Press Herald,* October 15, 1995, accessed December 2013.

[30] Mangione and Morreale, *La Storia,* 167.

[31] Henry Latini, telephone interview by author, September 11, 2013.

[32] Abby Zimet, "City Life: Diversity Revitalizes Area Little Italy Reborn,"*Portland Press Herald,* April 01, 1996, accessed December 30, 2013.

[33] DeSalvo, *Crazy in the Kitchen,* 131-137.

[34] Polito, *"Nobody Washes Me, I'm Italian!,"* 5.

[35] Ibid.,14.

[36] Kessner, *The Golden Door,* 26.

37 Kraut, *The Huddled Masses*, 30.

38 Kraut, *The Huddled Masses*, 32.

39 Banfield, "The Padrone, the Sojourners, and the Settlers."

40 1910 US Federal Census, Portland, ME.

41 Daniels, *Coming to America*, 195.

42 Lapomarda, *Italians in Maine*, 49.

43 Kessner, *The Golden Door*, 58.

44 Will Bartlett, "Dominic Candelmo Shoe and Hat Repairer, Native of Italy," *Portland Press Herald*, November 21, 1996, accessed December 30, 2013.

45 1910 US Census, Portland, ME.

46 1920 US Census, Portland, ME.

47 Polito, *Nobody Washes Me, I'm Italian!,*15.

48 Means 'fellow villager' in Italian.

49 Lindsay Tice, "Emmanuele Cobisi Laborer, Native of Sicily; Loved to Cook,"*Portland Press Herald*, November 17, 1999, accessed December 30, 2013.

50 *Lorello, DeSarno, Valente, Villacci Family History Book.*

51 1920 US Census, Portland, ME.

52 Polito, *Nobody Washes Me, I'm Italian!*, 15.

53 Iorizzo and Mondello, *The Italian-Americans*, 119.

54 Polito, *Nobody Washes Me, I'm Italian!*, 67.

55 Ibid., 64.

[56] Matt Byrne, "Anna E. Russo of Portland Dies at Age 83," *Portland Press Herald*, October 14, 2013, accessed October 14, 2013.

[57] "Lucia "Lucy" Pastore, 93," *Portland Press Herald*, January 23, 2001, accessed December 30, 2013,

[58] "Anthony Galli Self-employed Mason Contractor," *Portland Press Herald*, January 28, 1999, accessed December 31, 2013,

[59] United States, Census Bureau, *1930 US Census,* accessed January/February 2014, http://www.ancestry.com/.

[60] "James A. Maiorano Life Member of Knights of Columbus," *Portland Press Herald*, March 10, 1998, accessed December 30, 2013.

[61] "Dorothy Antonia Cavallaro Loving Mother, Grandmother," *Portland Press Herald*, January 25, 1996, accessed December 31, 2013.

[62] Andrew D. Russell, Ted Cohen, Will Bartlett, "All Four Mazziottis Are Still Together, Even after 50 Years," Portland Press Herald, June 22, 1996, accessed December 30, 2013.

[63] Ricci Family Interview.

[64] "Mary Fasulo Obituary," Portland Press Herald, March 19, 2013, accessed January 06, 2014.

[65] Lapomarda, *Italians in Maine*, 102.

[66] Violette, "Portland's Vine-Deer-Chatham Neighborhood 1920-1960."

[67] Puleo, *The Boston Italians*, 97.

[68] Ibid., 96.

[69] Ibid., 94.

[70] 1920 US Census, Portland, ME.

[71] DeSalvo, *Crazy in the Kitchen*, 64.

[72] Amoruso, *Being Italian,*10.

[73] 1920 US Census, Portland, ME.

[74] Emma Bouthillette, "Rose DeRice, 93, Hard-working, 'do-it-yourself' Mom," Portland Press Herald, October 06, 2010, accessed December 31, 2013.

[75] Joe Guidi and Allan Neff, interview by author, October 07, 2012.

[76] United States, Census Bureau, *1940 US Census*, accessed March 2014, http://www.ancestry.com/.

[77] Ibid.

[78] 1920 US Census, Portland, ME.

[79] Puleo, *The Boston Italians*, 97.

[80] Daniello, "Ghost Street," 105.

[82] "20th Century Statistics," United States Census, section goes here, accessed February 20, 2014, http://www.census.gov/prod/99pubs/99statab/sec31.pdf.

[83] Iorizzo and Mondello, *The Italian-Americans*, 130.

[84] Iorizzo and Mondello, *The Italian-Americans*, 130.

[85] Ibid., 56.

[86] Daniello, *Ghost Street*, 23.

[87] Iorizzo and Mondello, *The Italian-Americans*, 78.

[88] Abby Zimet, "Little Italy Area Reborn," *Portland Press Herald*.

[89] Iorizzo and Mondello, *The Italian-Americans*, 119.
[90] Rose Valente Carter, interview by author, November 2011.

[91] DeSalvo, *Crazy in the Kitchen*, 44.

[92] Ricci Family Interview.

[93]Mangione and Morreale, *La Storia*, 107.

[94] Lapomarda, *Italians in Maine*, 52.

[95] Ricci Family Interview.

[96] Ibid.

[97] Marie Maiorino, interview by author, September 29, 2012.

[98] "Mary Germani Breault Obituary," Concord Monitor, accessed December 30, 2013, http://www.concordmonitor.com/article/mary-breault-was-founder-of-italian-heritage-center-in-portland.

[99] "John A. Profenno a Founder of Italian Heritage Center," *Portland Press Herald*, April 02, 1999, accessed December 31, 2013.

[100] Banfield, "The Padrone, the Sojourners, and the Settlers."

[101] Ibid.

[102] Iorizzo and Mondello, *The Italian-Americans*, 77.

[103] Kessner, *The Golden Door*, 59.

[104] Daniello, *Ghost Street*, 27.

[105] *Portland City Guide 1940*, 123.

[106] *Portland City Directory*. (Portland, Me.: Tower Pub., 1925).

[107] 1910 US Census, Portland, ME.

[108] Ibid.

[109] 1930 US Census, Portland, ME.

[110] 1940 US Census, Portland, ME.

[111] Michael C. Connolly, *Seated by the Sea: The Maritime History of*

Portland, Maine, and Its Irish Longshoremen (Gainesville: University Press of Florida, 2010), pg. #94.

[112] Kessner, *The Golden Door*, 57.

[113] 1920 US Census, Portland, ME.

[114] 1930 US Census, Portland, ME.

[115] Ibid.

[116] 1940 US Census, Portland, ME.

[117] "Rose Valente Carter Interview"

[118] 1910, 1920, 1930, and 1940 US Censuses, Portland, ME.

[119] 1940 US Census, Portland, ME.

[120] 1920 US Census, Portland, ME.

[121] Daniello, "Ghost Street," 93.

[122] Michael Fixaris Interview.

[123] Joe Guidi and Allan Neff Interview.

[124] Mangione and Morreale, *La Storia*, 358.

[125] Joe Guidi and Allan Neff Interview.

[126] 1930 US Census, Portland, ME.

[127] Mangione and Morreale, *La Storia*, 335.

[128] Ibid., 304.

[129] Iorizzo and Mondello, *The Italian-Americans*, 69.

[130] 1910 US Census, Portland, ME.

[131] 1930 US Census, Portland, ME.

[132] Ibid.

[133] Mangione and Morreale, *La Storia*, 235.

[134] DeSalvo, *Crazy in the Kitchen*, 61.

[135] Ibid.,103.

[136] Rose Valente Carter Interview.

[137] *1925 Portland City Directory*, 1189.

[138] 1920 US Census, Portland, ME.

[139] *1925 Portland City Directory*, Ad Section, 79.

[140] Lapomarda, *Italians in Maine*, 122.

[141] *1925 Portland City Directory*, Ad Section, 71.

[142] 1940 US Census, Portland, ME.

[143] "Anthony Galli Self-employed Mason Contractor," *Portland Press Herald*, January 28, 1999, accessed December 31, 2013.

[144] Polito, *Nobody Washes Me, I'm Italian!*, 41.

[145] Ibid., 66.

[146] Ibid., 57.

[147] 1930 US Census, Portland, ME.

[148] Dennis Hoey, "Nunzi D'Alfonso, 79, Well-known Portland Contractor," *Portland Press Herald*, January 23, 2012.

[149] Dieter Bradbury, ""Redefining America," *The Portland Press Herald*.

[150] Joe Guidi and Allan Neff Interview.

[151] 1920 US Census, Portland, ME.

[152] "Hod," Merriam-Webster, section goes here, accessed April 02, 2014, http://www.merriam-webster.com/dictionary/hod.

[153] Lapomarda, *Italians in Maine*.

[154] *Lorello, DeSarno, Villacci, Valente Family History Book*.

[155] *1925 Portland City Directory*, Ad Section, pg. 68.

[156] *1951 City Directory*, Front Page Ad.

[157] "Joseph Pallotta, 78," *Portland Press Herald*, May 14, 2011, accessed February 15, 2011.

[158] *1945 Portland City Directory*, 106.

[159] Ibid., 1119.

[160] Iorizzo and Mondello, *The Italian-Americans*, 154.
[161] Mary Ann Ricci Butts," interview by author, July 13, 2013.

[162] Rose Valente Carter Interview.

[163] Kraut, *The Huddled Masses*, 151.

[164] Joe Guidi and Allan Neff interview.

[165] 1910 US Census, Portland, ME.

[166] The 1924 City of Portland Tax Records on Maine Memory Network have a photo of the bank. However, the bank does not show up in any of the Portland City Directory's during this time period, nor do those interviewed recall it.

[167] *1951 Portland City Directory*.

[168] *1925 Portland City Directory*, 1177.

[169] Ibid.

[170] Joe Guidi and Allan Neff Interview.

[171] Kraut, *The Huddled Masses*, 183.

[172] *Portland City Directory* (Portland, Me.: Tower Pub., 1929), pg. #1304.

[173] Amoruso, *Being Italian*, 10.

[174] Iorizzo and Mondello, *The Italian-Americans*, 110.

[175] Joe Guidi and Allan Neff interview.

[176] Lapomarda, *Italians of Maine*, 39.

[177] "Joe Guidi and Allan Neff Interview."

[178] Rose Valente Interview.

[179] Mangione and Morreale, *La Storia*, 164.

[180] Lapomarda, *Italians in Maine*, 49.

[181] Michael Fixaris Interview.

[182] *Lorello, DeSarno, Villacci, Valente Family History Book.*

[183] "Feature Obituary: Theresa Ciampi, 78, Featured in Ad for Amato's," Portland Press Herald, section goes here, accessed March 06, 2013.

[184] Abby Zimet, "Little Italy Reborn," *Portland Press Herald.*

[185] Steven G. Vegh, "An Italian (sandwich) Original to Be Torn down The Birthplace of Amato's Culinary Innovation Is No Oil Painting, Preservationists Agree.," *Portland Press Herald*, December 13, 1999, accessed December 30, 2013.

[186] John Mulkern, "Old St. Peter's Parish: Early Italian Families Settling in Portland," *The Wise Guide* (Portland, ME), July 18, 1975, Neighborhoods sec.

[187] *Portland City Directory* (Portland, Me.: Tower Pub., 1960), pg.94.

[188] *1964 Portland City Directory*, 36.

[189] Lapomarda, *Italians in Maine*, 50.

[190] "City Life: Diversity Revitalizes Area, LIttle Italy Reborn," *Portland Press Herald*

[191] Lapomarda, *Italians in Maine*, 45.

[192] "Teresa Ciampi Obituary," *Portland Press Herald.*

[193] "Joe Guidi and Allan Neff Interview"

[194] "Teresa Ciampi Obituary," *Portland Press Herald.*

[195] Lapomarda, *Italians in Maine*, 54.

[196] Dean Lunt, "Giving Back to the Neighborhood, A Growing Insurance Agency Saves a Piece of Portland History While Finding a New Downtown Location.," *Portland Press Herald*, October 26, 1999, accessed December 31, 2013.

[197] Emma Bouthillette, "Amedeo Reali, 83, Village Cafe Owner, Devoted to Family," *Portland Press Herald*, July 24, 2010, accessed August 28, 2013.

[198] Dean Lunt, "Giving Back to the Neighborhood," *Portland Press Herald.*

[199] Ricci Family Interview.

[200] Dean Lunt, "Giving Back to the Neighborhood," *Portland Press Herald.*

[201] Lapomarda, *Italians in Maine*, 85.

[202] Ibid.

[203] 1940 US Census, Portland, ME.

[204] "Albert Taliento," *Portland Press Herald.*

[205] "Camilla A. Gorham Foster Grandmother," *Portland Press Herald*, June 07, 1996, accessed December 30, 2013, http://libraries.maine.edu.ursus-proxy-

11.ursus.maine.edu/mainedatabases/authmaine.asp?url=http://search.proquest.com.ursus-proxy-11.ursus.maine.edu/docview/276748876?accountid=17222.

[206] Ricci Family Interview.

[207] 1930 US Census, Portland, ME.

[208] "Obituary of Michele Cremo, 97, former owner of Cremo's Bakery of Portland." (1993). *Maine News Index – Portland Press Herald.* http://digitalcommons.portlandlibrary.com/news_pph/1818.

[209] Joe Guidi and Allan Neff Interview.

[210] *1945 Portland City Directory*, 110.

[211] Ricci Family Interview.

[212] Matt Byrne, "Anna E. Russo of Portland Dies at Age 83," *Portland Press Herald,* October 14, 2013, accessed October 14, 2013.

[213] Kessner, *The Golden Door*, 95.

[214] Ibid., 96.

[215] 1910, 1920, 1930, 1940 US Federal Censuses, Portland, ME.

[216] Daniels, *Coming to America*, 19.

[217] 1920 US Census, Portland, ME.

[218] Ibid.

[219] 1920 US Census, Portland, ME.

[220] Carnevale, *A New Language,* 62.

[221] "Rose Valente Carter Interview."

[222] Mangione and Morreale, *La Storia*, 10.

[223] "Rose Valente Carter Interview."

[224] Joe Guidi and Allan Neff Interview.

[225] Iorizzo and Mondello, *The Italian-Americans*, 220.

[226] Lapomarda, *Italians in Maine*.

[227] *1940 Portland City Guide*, 115.

[228] *1951 Portland Street Directory*, 15.

[229] Lapomarda, *Italians in Maine*, 102.

[230] Mangione and Morreale, *La Storia*, 329.

[231] *1940 Portland City Guide*, 246.

[232] Lapomarda, *Italians in Maine*, 122.

[233] Ibid., 102.

[234] Ibid., 103

[235] Ibid., 102-3

[236] Joe Guidi and Allan Neff Interview.

[237] "St. Peter's to Honor Romani with Scholarship," *Portland Press Herald*, October 11, 1997, accessed December 31, 2013.

[238] Polito, *Nobody Washes Me, I'm Italian!*, 71.

[239] 1930 US Census, Portland, ME.

[240] Lapomarda, *Italians in Maine*, 107.

[241] Ibid.,103.

[242] Deirdre Fleming, "Italian Festival Tribute to Neighbors, Roots," *Portland Press Herald*, August 16, 2009.
[243] *1940 Portland City Guide*, 61.

[244] Ricci Family Interview.

[245] Mary Ann Ricci Interview.

[246] Meredith Goad, "For Portland's Italians, A Cookie Bonanza," *Portland Press Herald*, August 8, 2013, accessed August 8, 2013, http://www.pressherald.com/news/Baking-for-the-Bazaar.html?pagenum=full.

[247] John Rolfe, "St. Peter's 4-miler Has a Rich History, Some of It Serious," *Portland Press Herald*, July 20, 1997, accessed December 31, 2013.

[248] "Joseph L. Discatio," Portland Press Herald/Maine Sunday Telegram, section goes here, accessed December 30, 2013.

[249] Lapomarda, *Italians in Maine*, 113.

[250] Ibid., 115.

[251] David Evans, "Regenerating the Italian Race: The Italian Methodist Mission and the Americanization of Italian History," *Methodist History* 49, no. 3 (April 2011).

[252] Lapomarda, *Italians in Maine*, 113.

[253] 1930 US Census, Portland, ME.

[254] 1940 US Census, Portland, ME.

[255] *Greater Portland 350th Anniversary Publication: Portland's Past, Present & Future* (Portland, Me.: Material World Pub., 1982).

[256] Bauman, *Gateway to Vacationland*, 197.

[257] Ibid., 198.

[258] Colin Woodard, "Portland's Forgotten Heart," *The Bollard*, accessed March 30, 2014, http://thebollard.com/2007/12/06/portlands-forgotten-heart/.